INSIGHT INTO

EATING
DISORDERS

INSIGHT INTO

EATING DISORDERS

Helena Wilkinson

CWR

Copyright © Helena Wilkinson 2006

Published 2006 by CWR, Waverley Abbey House, Waverley Lane, Farnham, Surrey GU9 8EP England.

The right of Helena Wilkinson to be identified as the author of this work has been asserted by her in accordance with the Copyright, Designs and Patents Act 1988.

See back of book for list of National Distributors.

Unless otherwise indicated, all Scripture references are from the Holy Bible: New International Version (NIV), copyright © 1973, 1978, 1984 by the International Bible Society.

Other versions used:
Amplified: The Amplified Bible © 1987 Zondervan and the Lockman Foundation
CEV: Contemporary English Version © 1995 by American Bible Society
GNB: Good News Bible © 1996, 1971, 1976 American Bible Society
NASB: New American Standard Bible, © 1977, Lockman Foundation
TLB: The Living Bible, © 1971, 1994, Tyndale House Publishers

Concept development, editing, design and production by CWR

Printed in Slovenia by Compass Press

ISBN-13: 978-1-85345-410-3
ISBN-10: 1-85345-410-9

WAVERLEY ABBEY INSIGHT SERIES

The Waverley Abbey Insight Series has been developed in response to the great need to help people understand and face some key issues that many of us struggle with today. CWR's ministry spans teaching, training and publishing, and this series draws on all of these areas of ministry.

Sourced from material first presented over Insight Days by CWR at their base, Waverley Abbey House, presenters and authors have worked in close co-operation to bring this series together, offering clear insight, teaching and help on a broad range of subjects and issues. Bringing biblical understanding and godly insight, these books are written both for those who help others and those who face these issues themselves.

CONTENTS

FOREWORD

My personal and painful family experiences of eating disorders have convinced me of the need for clear understanding of, and help and teaching on, all aspects involved – including the spiritual dimension.

In this book, Helena Wilkinson brings together a breadth of theoretical knowledge, with a clear personal understanding of the experiential realities of the *disabling power* of eating disorders and a biblical view of the *enabling power* of God which can and does enable people to overcome them.

For our God-given life (physical, mental and spiritual) to be healthy, we need to take in the correct food to satisfy the hunger of our body and mind. But there is another hunger which we need to satisfy, a spiritual hunger, a hunger of the soul. Well-balanced and nutritious eating habits, physical, mental and spiritual, are therefore essential for healthy living. Eating disorders destroy this balance and can take the sufferer into a world of physical, psychological and spiritual disorder.

Helena's knowledge of this difficult subject, together with her compassion for sufferers, have nurtured the words penned within this book. They offer the reader a simple yet edifying insight into understanding, helping and working with people who have an eating disorder.

The work is skilfully reasoned, bringing a welcome and much-needed insight into the traumatic and often fatal world of eating disorders. This insight and her analysis of the subject make this book an excellent starting point for people who are seeking a biblical understanding of these extremely complex and often life-threatening conditions.

This work is therefore a fitting introduction for professional counsellors, therapists, pastoral workers, students and those who have an interest in, or want an understanding of, the subject. It also offers practical help for people who suffer with an eating disorder, or their families and friends.

Helena deals with the psychopathology of eating disorders, backing this with good research data and biblical validation. She fearlessly acknowledges the need of a heavenly Father who gave His Son in order that we might have abundant life. In this book, Helena emphasises the vital connection between the physical, psychological and spiritual dimensions of people, in relationship to eating disorders.

This book is a must for people with an eating disorder as it gives excellent practical and biblical helps, information and guidance. It would also be my desire to see people inspired to work with those who are suffering with eating disorders. Helena's work is an encouragement for prayer, and a motivation for further study and research into the spiritual dimension of dealing with precious souls who need the love, compassion and understanding of skilled clinicians, pastors and friends.

Dr Ralph J.C. Harkness

INTRODUCTION

In 1989 I was a student on the first Diploma course (One Year Institute in Christian Counselling) at Waverley Abbey House, and had the privilege of sitting under the devotional and counselling teaching of Selwyn Hughes and others. Towards the end of my counselling training Selwyn asked if I would consider joining the staff. For nearly four years I worked in both the editorial and counselling departments of CWR. It was during this time that I saw the birth of the Insight Days, including a day on eating disorders which, at times, I led.

When it was mentioned that a book on eating disorders should accompany the Insight Day, and form a part of a series of books, I thought it would be an excellent resource. People often find it beneficial following a teaching day to have material that can be further studied at home. Whilst I have written other books on eating disorders and related subjects, the advantage of *Insight into Eating Disorders* is that it is written in such a way as to follow the format of the Insight Day. I hope that it proves to be a support to many.

I first became involved in working with eating disorder sufferers some twenty years ago following the publication of *Puppet on a String*, my own story of suffering and recovery from anorexia. As I have walked the road with many sufferers and their families I have learned to see the world through their eyes, but not be drawn into what many describe as a hopeless situation. I have cried and rejoiced with sufferers. I have seen the terrible pain of a parent losing the life of a child due to an eating disorder; heard many a tragic story of why the eating disorder was developed; celebrated with those who were told they would never have a baby only to be proved wrong, and those who thought they would never recover and have!

My walk with others has involved female and male sufferers, children and adults (though for simplification I refer to the sufferer as 'she' in the book). I have seen young and old, one sibling and two, parent and child all caught in the throes of an eating disorder. Equally I have been aware of the vast array of people involved in a supportive role: parent, spouse, sibling, friend, counsellor, minister, GP, psychiatrist, CPN, etc. To all, I would say that I believe recovery is possible and I hope that the words of this book enable the process to become more possible. May the following scriptures be a comfort to you throughout the journey:

- ' ... I will not forget you! See, I have engraved you on the palms of my hands ... ' (Isa. 49:15–16)
- 'If you are attacked and knocked down, you will know that there is someone who will lift you up again ...' (Job 22:29, TLB)
- 'Do not be afraid – I will save you. I have called you by name – you are mine.' (Isa. 43:1, GNB)
- '... but with everlasting kindness I will have compassion on you ... ' (Isa. 54:8)
- 'The mountains and hills may crumble, but my love for you will never end ... ' (Isa. 54:10, GNB)

Helena Wilkinson
Gower, Swansea, 2006

CHAPTER 1

TIP OF THE ICEBERG

ACTIVITY UNDER THE SURFACE

'An eating disorder is like an iceberg,' I casually said one day, whilst talking with a group of eating disorder sufferers attending a course I was running.

'What do you mean?' someone piped up, apparently concerned that I might be inferring that eating disorder sufferers are hard and cold! I explained that with icebergs the part that is above the water surface, and visible to all, is small in comparison to that which lies, ominously, *below* the water's surface.

In fact, only about one ninth of the total mass of an iceberg projects above the water. There's not only a lot more under the water's surface than is obvious to the eye, but there has also been activity below the water for some time prior to the iceberg being noticed. Glaciers form on land due to an accumulation of snow over thousands of years and they 'creep' outward under their own weight. When the edge of a glacier advances into the ocean, some of the pieces break off and these are what we call icebergs.[1] In the same way, with an eating disorder, 'activity' under the surface and pain 'creeping' out forms what we see as an eating disorder.

JEMMA'S STORY

For Jemma, the tip of the iceberg was the overwhelming fear of being anywhere near a normal body weight, and the delight she took in feeling physically empty. Whilst others couldn't fail to see the massive iceberg in the middle of the ocean, Jemma couldn't keep her head above the water long enough to accept the obstruction it was causing; instead she was slowly being drowned by that which kept her submerged in the darkness below.

She was the older of two girls and always felt inferior to her sister. Her mum was very anxious and her dad was unemotional. She'd had a rough start in life, being born prematurely and being separated from the loving touch of her mother, so vital to a newborn baby. Her parents' relationship was not a happy one and Jemma often felt 'piggy in the middle'. The atmosphere at home was tense. Whilst still very young she was sexually abused by a close relative, which continued into her teens. At school, due to severe dyslexia and lack of adequate help, she was constantly told that she was 'sloppy'.

By her mid teens, Jemma was suffering from severe depression. She started to cut back on her eating and found that it made her feel in control when all else in her life controlled her. 'For a while things were better,' explained Jemma, 'then I started a summer job and was sexually assaulted. Something inside me snapped and I just wanted to disappear. It was then that the anorexia took a hold. I felt horribly threatened when others challenged my eating.'

THE DIFFERENT EATING DISORDERS

As we can see from Jemma's story, what is below the water's surface controls what happens above, and the issues could be relevant to any eating disorder. However, above the water's surface there are clear distinctions between the different eating disorders, as described in the *Diagnostic and Statistic Manual of Mental Disorders*:[2]

Diagnostic criteria for 307.1 Anorexia Nervosa

A. Refusal to maintain body weight at or above a minimally normal weight for age and height (e.g. weight loss leading to maintenance of body weight less than 85% of that expected; or failure to make expected weight gain during period of growth, leading to body weight less than 85% of that expected).

B. Intense fear of gaining weight or becoming fat, even though underweight.

C. Disturbance in the way in which one's body weight or shape is experienced, undue influence of body weight or shape on self-evaluation, or denial of the seriousness of the current low body weight.

D. In post-menarcheal females amenorrhea, i.e. the absence of at least three consecutive menstrual cycles. (A woman is considered to have amenorrhea if her periods occur only following hormone, e.g. estrogen, administration.)

Specify type:

Restricting Type: during the current episode of Anorexia Nervosa, the person has not regularly engaged in binge-eating or purging behavior (i.e., self-induced vomiting or the misuse of laxatives, diuretics, or enemas)

Binge-Eating/Purging Type: during the current episode of Anorexia Nervosa, the person has regularly engaged in binge-eating or purging behavior (i.e., self-induced vomiting or the misuse of laxatives, diuretics, or enemas)

Diagnostic criteria for 307.51 Bulimia Nervosa

A. Recurrent episodes of binge eating. An episode of binge eating is characterized by both of the following:

(1) eating, in a discrete period of time (e.g., within any 2-hour period), an amount of food that is definitely larger than most people would eat during a similar period of time and under similar circumstances

(2) a sense of lack of control over eating during the episode (e.g., a feeling that one cannot stop eating or control what or how much one is eating)

B. Recurrent inappropriate compensatory behavior in order to prevent weight gain, such as self-induced vomiting; misuse of laxatives, diuretics, enemas, or other medications; fasting; or excessive exercise.

C. The binge eating and inappropriate compensatory behaviors both occur, on average, at least twice a week for 3 months.

D. Self-evaluation is unduly influenced by body shape and weight.

E. The disturbance does not occur exclusively during episodes of Anorexia Nervosa.

Specify type:

Purging Type: during the current episode of Bulimia Nervosa, the person has regularly engaged in self-induced vomiting or the misuse of laxatives, diuretics, or enemas

Nonpurging Type: during the current episode of Bulimia Nervosa, the person has used other inappropriate compensatory behaviors, such as fasting or excessive exercise, but has not regularly engaged in self-induced vomiting or the misuse of laxatives, diuretics, or enemas

---

307.50 Eating Disorder Not Otherwise Specified

The Eating Disorder Not Otherwise Specified category is for disorders of eating that do not meet the criteria for any specific Eating Disorder. Examples include

1. For females, all of the criteria for Anorexia Nervosa are met except that the individual has regular menses.
2. All of the criteria for Anorexia Nervosa are met except that, despite significant weight loss, the individual's current weight is in the normal range.
3. All of the criteria for Bulimia Nervosa are met except that the binge eating and inappropriate compensatory mechanisms

occur at a frequency of less that twice a week or for a duration of less than 3 months.

4. The regular use of inappropriate compensatory behavior by an individual of normal body weight after eating small amounts of food (e.g., self-induced vomiting after the consumption of two cookies).

5. Repeatedly chewing and spitting out, but not swallowing, large amounts of food.

6. Binge-eating disorder: recurrent episodes of binge eating in the absence of the regular use of inappropriate compensatory behaviors characteristic of Bulimia Nervosa …

Compulsive eating, also known as binge eating disorder at present does not appear in the main text of DSM-IV, but rather in Appendix B: Criteria Sets and Axes Provided for Further Study.[3]

Research criteria for Binge Eating Disorder

A. Recurrent episodes of binge eating. An episode of binge eating is characterized by both of the following:

(1) eating, in a discrete period of time (e.g., within any 2-hour period), an amount of food that is definitely larger than most people would eat in a similar period of time under similar circumstances

(2) a sense of lack of control over eating during the episode (i.e., feeling that one cannot stop eating or control what or how much one is eating)

B. The binge-eating episodes are associated with three (or more) of the following:

(1) eating much more rapidly than normal

(2) eating until feeling uncomfortably full

(3) eating large amounts of food when not feeling physically hungry

(4) eating alone because of being embarrassed by how much one is eating

(5) feeling disgusted with oneself, depressed, or very guilty after overeating

C. Marked distress regarding binge eating is present.

D. The binge eating occurs, on average, at least 2 days a week for 6 months.

E. The binge eating is not associated with the regular use of inappropriate compensatory behaviors (e.g., purging, fasting, excessive exercise) and does not occur exclusively during the course of Anorexia Nervosa or Bulimia Nervosa.

ANOREXIA: THE QUEST FOR PURITY

When the anorexic sets out to cut back on her eating, she seems no different from anyone else who is dieting, but there is a subtle difference. For the dieter, eating less is only *one part* of her life and she diets to achieve physical attractiveness and health. For the anorexic, dieting is her *whole* life and she diets to achieve mastery over self. As she diets and discovers that it gives her a sense of achievement, she is motivated to keep losing weight when others would have stopped.

Although the anorexic declares that she is not hungry, apart from periods of loss of appetite through depression or the effects of prolonged starvation, she is often very hungry. In fact she is fascinated by food and feels triumphant in not giving in to the sensation; when she does give in she is filled with self-disgust at her weakness. It is not that the anorexic doesn't like food but that she fears losing control.

The anorexic also has a fear of weighing more than a certain weight (which is below average for her age and height). When she looks in the mirror a distortedly large figure stares back at her, and her face, filled with horror, gives away how much she detests the sight. She examines herself with great precision. As her hands glide over her body and she feels angular bones, she is reassured, but it is still not good enough.

Not eating causes restlessness and the anorexic may develop frantic exercise programmes, pushing her body to physical extremes. Soon she begins to develop rituals dictating that things must be done in a certain order and at a certain time; there is intense self-hatred when she fails to keep the harsh rules she has imposed. The lower her weight, the more impaired the anorexic's thinking becomes. Everything is seen in very black and white terms. She also loses much of her ability to be creative, expressive, imaginative, and to handle challenging situations.

As her weight drops, her drooping frame is no more than skin and bone. Shoulder blades and hip bones protrude. Her eyes are sunken and her skin pale. Her hands and feet feel perpetually cold and appear slightly purple due to poor circulation. On her arms, legs, back and face she may begin to develop a fine downy hair. She is frequently constipated, her skin is dry and her hair brittle. Her body is frail to hold. Her blood pressure is low and her heart rate slow. Over time her bones become like those of a much older person and she may develop osteoporosis.

Starvation causes irritability and selfishness and as the anorexic struggles with inner pain, and pushes against other people's control, she undergoes a personality change but she fears that if she lets go she will be faced with a surge of indulgence and agonising feelings. When people try to convince her that she is not well she sees it as a threat.

BULIMIA: THE LONGING FOR SATISFACTION

At times the bulimic can eat a normal meal without getting rid of the food. On other occasions she feels overcome by guilt and chooses to induce vomiting. She may starve herself all day and then crave food in the evening or raid the fridge in the night. The foods she buys for bingeing are those which she usually avoids eating. Sometimes her desperation to binge and vomit is so great that she doesn't care what she eats. Raw vegetables, raw meat, dry cereal, sweet, savoury and half-cooked food are all crammed in, one after the other, at great speed. The amount of calories consumed in one binge can be equal to what most people would eat in ten days.

Sometimes the bulimic feels disgusted by what she does and vows that she will never do it again. In a fit of desperation she forgets her promise and repeats the cycle. At other times there is a love-hate relationship: whilst she is disgusted that she could be capable of such behaviour, there is also a sense of excitement.

After her binge the bulimic feels heavy; her stomach is distended as though it may burst open. She is hot and sweaty and forces herself to vomit until she is sure that all the food has gone and she can return to a comforting state of emptiness. She feels tired and numb, but relaxed.

The bulimic may appear to have a puffy face due to swelling of the salivary glands, and be prone to throat infections. Perpetual vomiting can cause the oesophagus to bleed, and the enamel on the teeth to erode. A disturbance in the balance of electrolytes (potassium, sodium, magnesium and calcium, etc) affects both the bulimic and the anorexic. This can cause muscle weakness, numbness, kidney failure, and an erratic heartbeat. In a small number of people it can result in epileptic fits or heart failure.

Some bulimics and anorexics resort to taking large doses of laxatives. Drug and/or alcohol abuse is also not uncommon in people with eating disorders, particularly with the bulimic.[4] Self-harm, such as cutting and burning, is also common. Other forms of self-harm include bruising, biting, scratching, pulling out hair. Overdoses (which often are not serious suicide attempts but expressions of self-harm, confusion or desperation) are also common.

COMPULSIVE EATING: THE URGE FOR FULLNESS

To the compulsive eater, food means either overeating or dieting. It is also something about which she fantasises a great deal and which offers her comfort.

When the compulsive eater gives an account of what she has eaten that day she frequently fails to include certain foods. Some sufferers subconsciously believe that if they eat whilst standing up, driving or walking it 'doesn't count'. The compulsive eater may set out on a diet because of the pressure to be slim, but dieting feels like imprisonment and she often finds herself making up for those things which she has been deprived of.

The compulsive eater is so haunted by food that she might deliberately walk home a certain way in order to pass a food store. She makes excuses as she buys large quantities of provisions. 'I'll buy some cup cakes and éclairs for the kids,' she reasons – only the kids never see them as half are devoured on the way home and the remainder throughout the day. She eats guiltily and with speed, not really enjoying what she is eating, afraid that others might 'catch her'. Buying one item of food, especially sweet food, frequently leads to her buying more and more.

There are physical consequences for the compulsive eater, and not just because of being overweight. Current research is showing that people who diet and then regain their weight, and repeat the pattern over and over, are far more susceptible to gallstones. Overweight people are more likely to develop diabetes, raised blood cholesterol and to suffer from strokes and heart attacks.

Despite the knowledge of the physical damage, it does not stop people with compulsive eating, bulimia or anorexia continuing in the patterns. The compulsion to carry out the eating disorder is too strong. In the next few chapters we will explore what it is below the water's surface that acts with such force.

CHAPTER 2

BELOW THE WATER'S SURFACE

COMBINATION OF FACTORS

There is no single cause to an eating disorder. What lurks below the water's surface is often a combination of experiences, traumas and personality traits that together eventually result in the iceberg forming and forcing its way up into the open, until a jagged mound of ice (eating disorder) is blatantly obvious! Significant areas include:

1. Emotional hunger
2. Sexuality
3. Trauma
4. Family background

1. EMOTIONAL HUNGER

Everyone has needs which they long to have met, but when the neediness is intense this usually stems from having been deprived in some way as a child. Children require meaningful time and attention from their parents that is not interrupted by the parents' needs, does not demand back, and is not filled with anxiety. If needs are not met, or needs are seen as bad, weak, childish or selfish, then the person can be left with an empty void which then often gets filled through addictive and/or behavioural responses.

For the anorexic, who can't face the fact that she is still emotionally hungry, it becomes easier to pretend that she isn't hungry, physically or emotionally. Needs are a sign of weakness and she wants to achieve self-sufficiency. Marilyn Lawrence and Mira Dana believe that what the anorexic sees reflected in the mirror is not just her body, but a symbolic part of herself. It is the needy, demanding, yearning part which she so desperately tries to kill by starving her body, but which screams out to her, 'I want to be seen, noticed, listened to'. This may be the reason for her still seeing herself as enormous when really she is emaciated.[1]

Both the bulimic and the compulsive eater find it easier than the anorexic to admit to having needs, although the concept may evoke mixed reactions. The bulimic often feels her neediness, and then suddenly senses that she must push it away.

At one moment, she feels a sense of uncontrollable neediness ... She attempts to 'deal with' her emotional needs with food, and the violence and ferocity with which she eats gives us some indication of the strength of those needs and the desperation she feels to calm her disturbed feelings. As soon as she has eaten, the bulimic feels a compulsion to get rid of the food and to free herself of any reminder of her awful and terrifying needs.[2]

The compulsive eater

> ... very often feels needy and empty as though she desperately wants something inside her. However, instead of allowing herself to be fully aware of what those needs really are, she reaches for food and submerges her needs ... At the same time, she feels terribly guilty about her needs. She cannot perceive them and attempts to meet them in a straightforward way. Her needs are a source of shame, which is represented by her fat ...[3]

When she diets it is sometimes a desperate attempt to kill the hunger inside. But as she diets she gets more in touch with the emotional hunger and quickly returns to eating.

LOVE AND NURTURING

The need for love and nurture has become entangled with issues around food for many people with eating disorders. Lack of unconditional love as a child goes on affecting a person for as long as the deprivation is not faced and dealt with. In order to feel loved, a child needs not only to hear loving words, but to receive tenderness. The longing for love is also a longing for safety, protection and intimacy. Intimacy, for many sufferers, can feel frightening because it requires vulnerability. 'In early childhood, being vulnerable usually resulted in feeling abandoned and alone.'[4]

Some sufferers feel the intensity of the need for love as though they are still children. Many are longing for childhood needs to be met through the nurturing and validation by others and

27

have not yet learnt the importance of nurture and validation by self. Hence eating disorders are more often than not responses to other people not fulfilling what the person sees as essential to their emotional well-being.

When someone is in pain, food is a quick and easy form of being nurtured, but if it isn't food that a person is longing for, then food will never satisfy. Doctors Donald Klein and Michael Liebowitz, following extensive research, discovered that when someone is in love their body produces a chemical called phenylethylamine. Chocolate is loaded with that very same substance.[5]

SELF-WORTH AND SECURITY

Unmet emotional needs also affect self-worth and security. What we believe others think of us often rules how we feel about ourselves and how we act towards others. The conclusions we come to about ourselves are formed at a very early age. 'Significant adults, such as parents, older siblings and teachers become the "mirrors" in which young children see themselves.'[6]

'People with a good self-esteem are comfortable with themselves. They accept themselves, including their shortcomings. This acceptance doesn't stop them from making changes; it frees them to do so. They are able to have a balanced estimate of themselves. They can be fully in touch with their emotions, but not controlled by them.'[7]

When people have a low self-worth they often suffer from depression. They see themselves negatively; life negatively (demanding and unfair); the future negatively (without hope).[8] Other long-term effects include stress, guilt, anger, jealousy, loneliness, lack of intimacy, feelings of failure, and a distorted picture of God. Eating disorders are one way in which people compensate for their poor self-worth. Other ways can be through: excessive shyness, drawing attention to themselves, putting themselves down, boasting, always having to be right, suspicion and criticism, rigid thinking, aggression, overwork.[9]

Many eating disorder sufferers do not have a strong sense of self-worth and security, and the eating disorder is used to fill the gap.

The anorexic's body-size represents the way she feels about herself. She views herself as so small and insignificant that if she existed in a normal body she would rattle around. Not eating is both a visible way of explaining to the world that she is 'a nobody' and, at the same time, a desperate attempt to regain some worth through rigid self-control. The bulimic sees herself as bad inside. Her self-worth is measured in terms of being in control of her eating. Her worth will go up and down depending on how 'good' she has been, and how she looks. For the compulsive eater who hates herself, stuffing herself with sweet foods that are not good for her is very easy. She may feel that she doesn't even deserve nice food, served on a plate, and eaten politely.

For many women, especially those who go on to develop an eating disorder, self-image (the way we see ourselves) centres around body-image (the picture we have of our bodies).[10]

2. SEXUALITY

Whichever eating disorder a person goes on to develop, there can be an element of being unsure about how to handle sexuality, and food and weight are used as a means of expressing this confusion.

Anorexics and bulimics are very critical of their bodies. At puberty they may examine their changing shape and, in shock, think, 'Help! I'm fat. I must get rid of it'. Some see this as the need to be slim whilst others equate weight gain with sexual expectation from others. Puberty often scares a sufferer because changes are happening to her over which she has no control. These changes are often taking place at the same time as the need for control becomes all-important in her life. Her fear drives her to take a drastic measure such as starvation.

Anorexia is sometimes associated with a fear of growing up and sexual maturity. The pre-anorexic child is said to be behind her peers in terms of emotional and sexual adjustment, and it is not uncommon for her to feel ashamed of the bodily changes taking place at puberty. The idea of getting rid of the signs of sexual development, such as fat around the hips, and putting an end to menstruation, which is a monthly reminder of adult responsibility and leaves her feeling dirty, can be appealing.

In the mind of bulimics, bulimia and sexual activity are closely linked; they may use intercourse or masturbation as a means of thwarting a bulimic attack, or bingeing to the point of sedation to lessen their sexual feelings.[11] There is a hunger for love which is sometimes mistakenly thought of as a hunger for sex.

Like bulimics, compulsive eaters may sometimes use food to satisfy their sexual needs. Being fat also stops a person from having to compete to be sexually attractive. In one group it was seen as providing sexual protection. Fat prevents them from considering themselves as sexual.[12] To be slim can mean that the compulsive eater's sexuality is too exposed, which may feel very uncomfortable. 'She imagines that if she loses the weight she will be losing a protective coating against the world.'[13]

SEXUAL ABUSE
A fairly high percentage of victims of sexual abuse go on to develop an eating disorder.

The home of an abused child can set her up for abuse. There is distance in relating. Two of the factors which are essential to a happy home would have been absent: the sense of being enjoyed for who she is rather than for what she does, and the opportunity to develop separateness from the other members of the family. The child might have carried adult burdens; have been led to believe that certain feelings are wrong, crazy, or non-existent. The atmosphere in the home might have been demanding, conservative, or rule bound; the highest value being loyalty to protect the family. The child would, to some extent, have felt empty, committed to pleasing people, and would not have had clear boundaries.[14]

Feeling hungry for emotional attention, the child may take whatever is offered and find herself a victim of abuse.

The effects of sexual abuse are many. The person can feel guilty, dirty, rejected, disgusted and different. The survivor often believes that it was her own desire to be cared for, wanted, hugged and loved which led to the abuse. She 'feels deceived by her body; the body is the enemy, and were it not for the body there would never have been a problem'.[15] The most powerful emotions which are carried around are shame, anger and powerlessness. The child who is abused feels powerless, and she continues to do so as an adult. She believes that she does not have choices and that she cannot change her circumstances. She doesn't value herself enough to choose to walk away from situations where people treat her badly, and as a result she very easily finds herself in ongoing abusive situations.

Eating disorders serve a function in response to sexual abuse by:

Creating protection. By becoming obsessed with food and by forming a relationship with food where it, rather than people, brings comfort, the survivor has a greater chance of protecting herself from being wounded by others. For the anorexic and the compulsive eater, changing her body to being unattractive to the opposite sex also limits her chance of being involved in an unwanted sexual relationship.

Dealing with feelings. Rage, guilt, shame and pain must be deadened and eating disorders provide a way to lessen painful emotions. In addition to the eating disorder, self-harm often becomes a way of dealing with pain or helping to shift from one feeling to another. Cutting or burning is a means of making visible what is going on inside and overdoses can be attempts to 'kill' the pain.

Shifting the focus. For as long as the sufferer concentrates on food and weight, she can shift the focus from the devastation of the abuse. By concentrating on the behaviour of the eating disorder, the pain of what happened to her does not need to be faced. For someone afraid to feel the full impact of abuse, the concept of the focus being directed elsewhere is very attractive.

Neutralising dirt. Many people who have been abused feel dirty, and eating disorders serve the function of neutralising this feeling. Purging and starving both create a sense of cleansing, and eating disorders are often accompanied by obsessive compulsive behaviour focused around cleanliness and tidiness.

Establishing control. Any form of abuse puts the person in a powerless position. Eating disorders become one way of gaining a feeling of control through what she does to her body. The anorexic needs to take control of her body to try to get rid of the terrible flaw she feels exists. The bulimic and compulsive eater experience lack of control in order to reassert control over the body.

3. TRAUMA

Many people with eating disorders have gone through trauma prior to the eating disorder. It is not uncommon for there to be a two-year gap between the trauma occurring and the eating disorder developing. Traumas might include: separation/ abandonment, bullying, physical, emotional and sexual abuse, death of a close relative, separation/divorce of parents, disability, witnessing an assault, violence, etc.

The eating disorder serves the purpose of coping with the trauma(s) but besides an eating disorder other disorders may also be present, such as:

- Post-traumatic Stress Disorder
- Borderline Personality Disorder
- Acute Stress Disorder
- Depression
- Dissociative Identity Disorder
- Obsessive Compulsive Disorder

One of the means of identifying whether there is unprocessed trauma in a person's life is to consider what other patterns of behaviour and belief systems are in operation besides the eating disorder. The following list[16] is used by The Ross Institute Trauma Program as a means of assessing whether someone is suitable for their trauma programme, but it can equally be a guide for considering if there is still unresolved trauma in someone with an eating disorder.

1. Suicidal Ideation *(Consideration of suicide as a realistic option)*
2. A pattern of out-of-control and self-injurious behavior.
3. Self-destructive addictions:
    a. Dual Diagnosis
    b. Eating Disorders
    c. Self Mutilation
    d. Sexual Addictions
4. Intrusive thoughts, images, feelings and nightmares.
5. Flashbacks.
6. Extensive co-morbidity/multiple diagnoses.
7. Inability to tolerate feelings or conflicts.
8. Intense self-blame and feeling unworthy.
9. Staying stuck in the victim or perpetrator roles.
10. Disorganized attachment patterns.
11. Black and white thinking and other cognitive distortions.
12. Pathological dissociation.

Where there is trauma, it is important that the sufferer receives the right type of help to work through the past. Without appropriate forms of therapeutic interaction further damage can be done.

4. FAMILY BACKGROUND

The family background in and of itself is not the cause of an eating disorder, but aspects of the sufferer's background may well contribute to the developing of an eating disorder.

The families of those with eating disorders provide well for their children in terms of physical, material and educational needs, but the area often lacking is the meeting of emotional needs. Aspects of the family background which are relevant to eating disorders include:

- Communication
- Shame
- Boundaries
- Negative feelings

COMMUNICATION

The child who goes on to develop an eating disorder uses behaviour rather than words to communicate needs and feelings, because generally non-direct communication has been role-modelled in the family.

Researchers who were sent into anorexic families reported that they felt uncomfortable when the whole family was together; they had to be careful not to 'make waves'.[17] Pre-anorexic children come across as needing their parents more, and being very aware of the conflicts and neglects. They are vulnerable, compliant and take criticism and 'put downs' very seriously.[18]

> Prior to the anorexia developing, the child has been seen as good, obedient and loveable, with few problems. Yet it is not uncommon for her to be feeling intense inner anguish. The child tends to feel that she is not good enough in that she does not live up to 'expectations' or that she could be in danger of losing her parents' love and consideration. But she conceals her discontent, behaving as if she were happy. She feels 'undeserving', 'unworthy' and 'ungrateful'. She often complains that she has received too many privileges and feels burdened by having to live up to such 'specialness'.[19]

A study of bulimics indicated that the relationship with their parents was very poor. The sufferers felt they were shown little attention, and that their parents did not spend much time with them, did not know them well, and tended to be reserved and unemotional – there was little affection expressed within the family. The sufferers would have liked to have communicated more with their parents; they felt they did not have very meaningful conversations with their mothers. A number of sufferers said that as teenagers, they had not spent much time with their fathers.[20]

SHAME
Shame, which is a feeling of being defective as a person, is often significant in eating disorder families. Maxine West, a psychologist, points out that in these families it is extremely important that members look and act appropriately. Many 'rules' exist ... and a 'front' is created and outsiders see and interact with this 'front', not with what is *really* happening in the family. This can affect the child's sense of reality. Control is imperative to survival.[21] Value and acceptance are based on performance and members are afraid of what the existence of a problem 'says' about them.[22]

BOUNDARIES
Each family has its own set of boundaries and out of these a child begins to learn who she is as an individual and where she stands in relation to family members and outsiders. Marilyn Lawrence and Mira Dana indicate two extremes of boundary problems which occur in eating disorder families. In one type of family, privacy and being an individual are highly prized and it may be difficult for the members to feel close to each other, to share, or to truly relate. In another type of family, the need for privacy is experienced as rejection. It is considered that everything should

be shared; everyone has to know all about everyone else. Even feelings are family property; it can be impossible for one member to be upset without affecting the whole family.[23]

Salvador Minuchin has found anorexic families to be over-involved, overprotective, not willing to change, and tending to avoid conflict.[24] Palazolli indicates that the child, rather than the conflict between the parents, becomes the family problem. This focus on the child's symptoms serves to *express* as well as *avoid* the unresolved conflicts existing between the parents.[25] If conflict is not openly expressed, the child never learns how to resolve it, and will remain frightened of situations where even differing opinions are spoken. The anorexic's goals become approval and love rather than knowledge or competence. She will develop an obsessional concern for perfection, resulting in low self-esteem. She will also struggle with extreme self-consciousness, making it difficult for her to form relationships outside the family and creating increased dependency upon the approval of her parents.[26]

It is reported that despite the children of compulsive eating families being intelligent, they cling to their mothers. Their mothers still do things for them, way after the children are capable of doing things for themselves. Mothers also compensate for insecurity by excessive feeding, so food has an exaggerated emotional meaning and can be a substitute for love, security and satisfaction. … As an adolescent, the sufferer often thought that her father's interest was only in how well she looked or how successful she was, and not in what she valued or how she felt.[27]

NEGATIVE FEELINGS

How negative feelings are handled in the family can be a part of the chain of events that lead to the developing of an eating disorder.

Not dealing with emotions teaches the child that she must suppress how she really feels in order to be 'acceptable'. The eating disorder family may find it hard to cope with certain feelings, such as anger, and the members are not encouraged to discuss how they feel. The parents may discount their children's feelings by stating that whatever has happened can't be that bad, or quell their emotions by inferring that children shouldn't feel that way.

> Members aren't allowed to question the family rules or to voice thoughts or feelings that conflict with these rules. Disagreement is met with rejection. Children from this type of home don't learn to communicate openly and directly. They don't learn that one can disagree with someone else and still have the person's respect and acceptance ... they become afraid to express themselves, until eventually they don't have a clue as to who they are or how they feel. They learn to avoid conflict at any price, to swallow 'unacceptable' thoughts and feelings so as not to upset others, and constantly to fear rejection.[28]

The children can come away with the sense that they are not loved and accepted, or if they are, it is only if, or when, they perform. They can feel that they are not valuable or worthwhile. They often feel very alone and as though they do not really belong anywhere.[29]

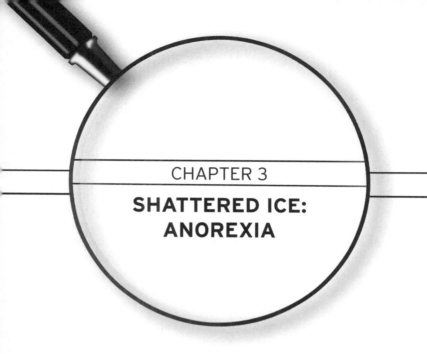

CHAPTER 3

SHATTERED ICE: ANOREXIA

ESCAPING PAIN

Anorexia is not really the problem but rather a way of coping with a whole series of problems. For various reasons the person feels unsafe, and she discovers that through not eating and pursuing thinness she is in a better position to handle her world. Traumatic events may not necessarily have happened to her – life itself can feel traumatic.

The anorexic usually doesn't know what to do with pain or ordinary feelings such as neediness, anger, frustration, jealousy and vulnerability. John Bradshaw considers that the anorexic *renounces* her emotions by refusing to eat, and that food seems to equal feelings.[1] She believes that she should have only 'nice' feelings. To one struggling with crushing emotional pain, a loss of feeling can seem very attractive. Not eating produces a 'high' which masks the emptiness, and any feelings which do remain appear to get transferred to issues around food, such as anger over having eaten more than the 'allowed' calories for the day.

HIDING CONFLICT

The behaviour patterns of the anorexic distract her from confronting her true feelings. For instance, anger is pushed down and not eating becomes her one means of expressing her anger. She may be hurt, disappointed and angry but because she does not know how to resolve conflict, facing these feelings is too dangerous and she feels that she must destroy them. The anorexic is rarely aware that she is angry for any reason other than being made to eat or having 'broken' her own 'rules'.

If anger has not been allowed to be expressed it becomes an alienated part of the person. The person feels shame whenever she is angry. This part of her must be disowned or severed. Blocking off the emotional energy of anger, she becomes a people-pleaser. All her feelings, needs and drives are bound by shame. When the shame has been completely internalised, nothing about her feels OK – she feels flawed and inferior. She turns her eyes inwards and scrutinises every minute detail of behaviour, creating a tormenting self-conscience. With parts of her severed and alienated there is a sense of unreality; of never quite belonging.[2]

ESTABLISHING IDENTITY

Anorexia often starts at a time in a person's life when she is questioning who she is, whether she really matters and what life is all about. There is an intensity in the questions being asked and she has a panic-stricken feeling that there are no answers. 'Yes, she is damaging herself; yes, she could die or do herself irreparable harm, but the alternative for her is to give in and be nothing'[3] and the fear of lack of identity is huge.

A loss of identity can also develop when a child is too controlled by another person or made to feel that she must become what someone else wants her to be. For fear of losing approval, the anorexic may not have been through times of normal teenage 'rebelling'. She may be searching for the meaning of life or be wrestling with her position in the family or with her peers, and so the anorexia creates a form of identity by giving her a sense of being in charge of her own life.

WANTING INDEPENDENCE

A crisis over independence arises out of the fact that other people have defined how the sufferer should be. Lack of individuality leads to over-submissiveness, non-assertiveness and difficulty in making decisions or forming opinions. It is hard for the anorexic to know what she wants and doesn't want because mostly other people have indicated what she *ought* to want. Some of the rules and rituals she creates concerning what she will eat, and when, enable her to feel that she is making choices and decisions about preferences. In controlling her food and weight, she is making a statement about independence. Yet, in regressing to a childlike state physically, she is showing that she cannot cope with independence.

The anorexic has usually not been brought up in an environment where she has been able to be silly or make a mess and still feel accepted. She has rarely experienced what it is like to be hurt and retreat into embracing arms without overreaction or overprotectiveness. Being with people who are both silly and tease her feels extremely painful. Peer groups involve both silliness and teasing, so she often stands on the edge of the group.

Peter Lambley comments that, for the anorexic, 'not normal' means having the basis of her creativity and energy cut away and pushed into empty, superficial rituals which leave her lonely and disgruntled. She hates herself for needing attention, for whining and for being a nuisance. She goes on protesting but feels bad and ugly.

> There is no physical contact, no emotionality, no challenge, no childishness, no outside contact. The anorexic girl senses these things and learns (while her peers are busy enjoying life) that all these needs are signs of inadequacy or weakness. To the loneliness is added a deep sense of guilt and hurt: a massive and growing nausea and self-disgust. And no way to solve it.[4]

FEARING RESPONSIBILITY

Responsibility and decision-making are seen by many anorexics as requiring a level of self-confidence and assertiveness which the sufferer feels she doesn't have.

> It is not so much a question of not knowing what she wants; she doesn't of course but that is the lesser problem; the major problem is that she does not know what she ought to want. For most people, need determines choice but what the anorexic may need barely concerns her since she is usually convinced that she deserves and therefore should have – nothing.[5]

The anorexic tends to be sensitive and a deep thinker who takes things very seriously and personally. She feels responsible for the whole world and is burdened by events around her. Contact with the world may have been minimal in her family, or the world may have been talked about as somewhere fraught with danger. When she is faced with the prospect of stepping outside her home, it is like putting a foot into an unknown jungle and she reasons it is safer to lock herself into her anorexic fantasies, even if at times it feels like prison.

DESIRING PERFECTION

The desire to overcome that which is not 'nice' and to attain purity is very strong in the anorexic. Marilyn Lawrence and Mira Dana see this as a quest for *moral perfection*.[6] The meeting of ordinary needs, such as hunger and comfort, is regarded as a sign of moral failure. Anything which falls below the anorexic's standard is 'bad'. Unlike most people who, in viewing themselves or life experiences, have a sliding scale of varying degrees of goodness and badness, the anorexic has only two points – 'exceptionally good' or 'thoroughly bad'.

Perfection is shown in high standards for herself and in the way she relates to others. Her determination and drive, which are very strong, can be both positive and negative. These usually mean that the anorexic achieves well, but also that when most people would give up she will still be pushing herself, resulting in extreme pressure. Being average means not being good enough and feeling like 'a nothing'. The anorexic's striving for perfection becomes concentrated on the body, and starving herself gives her the sense that she can achieve in a way in which others can't.

NEEDING CONTROL

The anorexic's harsh judgments of herself, her low self-esteem and her extreme sensitivity leave her vulnerable to the control of other people. Her experience is of being pressured by everyone with whom she comes into contact. Other people's needs, feelings and expectations automatically become obligations upon her. Because she feels there is no way of resolving the conflict which these needs and expectations create, she feels trapped and confused.[7] If she can't control her circumstances she controls herself within those circumstances. Not eating becomes the only way she knows how to take control.

Anorexia gives a sense of power in a life that has known the struggle of powerlessness. Whether that powerlessness has been through control, trauma or peer pressure, there now exists the need to feel in control and never experience that sense of powerlessness again.

Loss of control is considered as 'failure' and greatly feared. The control is not merely in connection with food and weight but over every area of life. There exists the fear that the minute the slightest control is lost, all control will disappear and she will be forced to the depths of self-indulgence. Guilt acts as a deadly reminder that indulgence, of even the smallest amount, is the ultimate 'sin'; and 'giving in' is a sign of complete and utter uselessness.

Losing weight is proof to the anorexic that she is able to exert willpower over the less desirable things in life, such as indulgence and feelings. It is a way of declaring that she does not need anything, especially nourishment and people. Yet inside she is crying out for the very things she is rejecting.

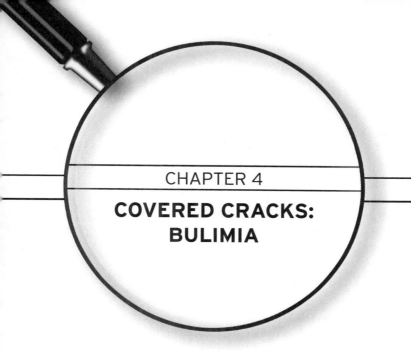

CHAPTER 4

COVERED CRACKS: BULIMIA

CONFLICTING IMAGES

There is a split between the part of the bulimic which is very much in control and is a coper and the part which is dependent and a non-coper. She feels ashamed of the non-coping part of herself which she tries to shut away from others. The nature of the illness is one of covering up. It is about hiding the truth, hiding feelings, hiding food. Everything is done in secret – the eating, the vomiting, the tears.

The bulimic is trying hard to take control of her life but is also in a great deal of conflict. She wants to present herself as someone who is strong and yet inside she feels needy and emotionally hungry. To observe the behaviour of the bulimic – the desperate craving, the rapidity with which food is often consumed, and the secretiveness – is to see that the conflict is 'about having a clean, neat, good, un-needy appearance which conceals behind it a messy, needy, bad part, which must be hidden away'.[1]

Some bulimics have referred to the messy part as 'the monster within'. The worse the bulimia becomes the bigger the monster grows and the greater the fear that one day it may burst out of their skin for the whole world to see. In addition to being emotionally symbolic, the bulimic pattern can be a way of physically releasing tension brought about through inner conflict, family problems, loneliness, stress, anxiety and depression.

SHIFTING RELATING

By consuming enormous amounts of food the bulimic is saying 'I am desperately needy'. By vomiting it all out she proclaims 'I reject it all. I am terrified of actually having any of my needs met'. She can show a similar attitude in her relationships. She will often find herself driven into a relationship by her emotional needs but later puts an end to it because of fear.[2]

Life for the bulimic feels like a vicious circle. She wants to achieve high standards, she wants perfection in relationships, but she feels it is impossible to maintain these standards. She binges instead. Just as the bulimic feels out of control with food, she can also feel out of control in relationships and with spending money.

Underneath the bulimic's facade there exists a hollow aloneness and hunger to be cared for. But she is afraid that once she allows people to touch the part of her which longs to be treasured, they will be sucked into her vacuum of hunger. She feels so desperate and so much in need that if she dares to expose her desires too much she fears they will consume everything and everyone in sight. The bulimic usually reasons that she must only allow herself to experience these longings at certain moments – these are the occasions when she indulges in the world of food.

Bingeing and vomiting is her one time of coming face to face with all she longs for, taking in more and more and more until full and satisfied and fit to burst. But she must only have all she longs for for a short while, then it must be emptied from her so that she can carry on with life, able and in control. It is hard for the bulimic to understand that everyone has longings and that it's OK both to feel and admit to these longings. For her the feeling is dangerous.

The 'mess' she feels she makes in her chaotic eating can be projected onto friendships and, just as food is taken in and thrown out, friendships may be formed and dropped quite quickly. The pain inside is unbearable as she feels, yet again, that she must escape from someone with whom she considers she has 'blown it'. She often seeks relationships where there is a lack of commitment, with someone who does not give of themselves emotionally. She also finds it hard to be committed herself and may opt for a relationship from which she can easily break away, making her feel safer.

It is not uncommon for the bulimic to feel confused over intimacy or closeness. She longs to feel close but dreads the thought that when other people get to know her they will discover the 'bad' part of her. This means that she rarely experiences herself as deeply loved or nurtured by anyone. She lives in fear of the other person taking her over in a relationship, and of losing her identity. At other times she feels the urge to take control. Wanting to be cared for and then running before others have a chance to really get to know her creates a 'pull–push' style of relating.

DESTROYING LOVE

The part of herself which the bulimic considers she needs to get rid of in her vomiting is

> … the part of the self which is able to indicate what it is that the self really needs, feels, wants, likes, dislikes, yearns for. She has no access to this part of herself, and instead she becomes dominated by a series of 'oughts', 'shoulds' and 'musts': a set of external rules which she has carried with her since childhood and which bear little or no relation to what she wants or likes. Thoughts replace feelings; oughts, shoulds and shouldn'ts replace real emotional or physical preferences.[3]

Not only is the bulimic trying to create a perfect image, but she is also searching for a perfect love, a love which will enable her to feel differently about herself and her circumstances. Yet love in relationships never fully satisfies her. To be loved by others is to risk letting the other person see the 'ugly' part of her, to be taken over by the other person or to lose control. To love others is to feel the desire to consume the other person, take total control and not allow them any breathing space. Her hunger drives her to continue looking for love, but nothing ever seems to satisfy. Nothing can be held onto for any length of time.

The bulimic may be searching in adult relationships for what she felt she failed to find in her childhood relationships. In fact this is true of all eating disorders.

> Being bulimic provides her with a way of avoiding seeing and experiencing that yearning for love and approval and the emptiness and self-hatred perpetuated by the disappointment of not getting it. Overeating and vomiting fills up the empty space, while at the same

time actively symbolising how impossible she finds it to take in and keep in anything good. The bulimia soon becomes for her the excuse, her reason, for not being loved.[4]

SPLITTING FEELINGS

The 'bad' part of the sufferer is seen as that which contains 'bad' feelings and weakness. These are feelings and experiences which she has been brought up to believe are not acceptable or must be kept hidden from other people, such as hostility, anger, sadness, sexual desire and neediness.

The way in which some people deal with 'bad' feelings is to separate them from the 'good' feelings and not allow them to be part of the person they show to the outside world. The bulimic splits off her 'bad' feelings, believing that if she didn't have bulimia she wouldn't have these feelings. She finds it extremely hard both to see and accept that negative feelings are a part of her.

> The bulimia is a separate part of the sufferer which encapsulates 'the problems' in her life, like a bubble where all the unacceptable, hated and feared aspects of herself are lodged. Her 'badness' is pushed away and centred on her bulimia. All her bad, needy, angry, dependent aspects become attached to the bulimia, so that they are not directly experienced. The bathroom is the one place she will allow her 'mess' to spill over.[5]

Bulimia takes an enormous amount of energy; energy which would be used to express feelings is used to keep them down.

> Instead of feeling distress, she feels an uncontrollable appetite. These feelings throw her into chaos and she tries to satisfy herself by

cramming food into her mouth. As soon as she has eaten and comes into touch with her needy, violent, devouring self, she is filled with guilt and feels an urgent desire to rid herself of what she has eaten. The end result of the bulimia, the eating and vomiting, is that the woman feels empty and entirely without needs. This is precisely the feeling she is seeking … In a limited way, bulimia achieves for her what she wants. The split-off, unwanted part of herself is contained in the symptom, leaving the rest of her life free from trouble and distress. The problem with this solution is that she has a continual sense of cheating, of achieving everything in a fraudulent way. Everything she actually does is undermined for her by the means she uses to achieve it.[6]

CHAPTER 5

FILLED VOIDS: COMPULSIVE EATING

MASKING PROBLEMS

The attitude towards herself and towards other people often shows itself in the eating patterns of the compulsive eater. By eating large quantities of food she can be expressing her need for more. Not just more food – more care, more understanding, more comfort, more time, more friends, more freedom, more of whatever she feels deprived of at that moment.

Compulsive eating can be a lonely and depressing affair in which loving and relying on food can feel safer than loving and relying on people. Food is always close at hand when the sufferer is hurting – people are not. Food does not retaliate, challenge, have expectations or want anything in return – people might. Food helps to mask problems and to push down unwanted emotions. Compulsive eating can be used, without the person realising, to avoid the fact that her life is disappointing, comfort her when other people cause hurt, hide the vulnerable real part of her or flee handling responsibility. Food is eaten to ease frustration and tension and to disguise insecurity.

The compulsive eater's solution to *any* pain or discomfort is food – to have something in the mouth and to fill up the gaping hole. When she is eating, the compulsive eater can feel warm, safe and strong. For a while, at least, she can forget about her hurts and about reality. She eats to anaesthetise painful feelings and may become agitated if anyone disturbs her special time with food. She eats as a means of coping with uncomfortable feelings and in response to positive feelings. She eats when she is bored or if she is feeling out of control. There is hardly a situation or emotion that does not demand food. 'Both a sense of power and a sense of powerlessness are felt as hunger.'[1]

The compulsive eater may also turn to food when: she can't accomplish her 'too-high' goals; things don't go right; people don't do what they should; events don't run smoothly; people don't like her behaviour. In short, the compulsive eater eats because the world doesn't operate the way it would if it were perfect. In addition she may:

- minimise her successes
- maximise her failures
- see only problems ahead
- blame others when she falls short[2]

SEEKING RELIEF

One of the warning signs of compulsive eating is that sufferers 'have a low tolerance for "negative" feelings (anger, sadness, fear, etc.)'.[3] The answer to this for many people is instant relief: 'I hurt and so I must find something which will take that hurt away *now*.' Little else is more instant in providing comfort than sweet food, especially chocolate.

The patterns of seeking relief from negative feelings and experiences through food are often learned early in childhood. The child who was always given sweets as a pacifier when she hurt herself or to keep her quiet may, in adult life, easily turn to food for comfort. It is not unusual for sufferers to come from homes where the parents gave their children food, or deprived them of it, for reasons that had no relation to the child's sensations of hunger.

The parents might have struggled to show affection except by the gift of food, or it may have been offered to distract the child, even tranquillise her, by an otherwise occupied mother. Such mothers will have deprived the child of the ability to learn for herself whether she is truly hungry. When the child grows up she will have suffered two fundamental gaps in her education: not being able to recognise real hunger and being deprived of a feeling of independence.[4] The ache of emotional emptiness gets translated into pangs of physical emptiness. She also finds it hard to perceive that pain is a part of life which will not always go when she wants it to, and that gratification, at times, may need to be deferred.

When in pain or under stress, the natural human reaction is to look for a means of escape. Food can act as a tranquilliser:

> ... each time a person eats, the brain stimulates some of the neurochemicals, the endorphins, which are natural pain-killers, relaxants and pleasure stimulators ... they are a God-given part of our mechanism, and certain activities stimulate them, such as laughter, sexual excitement, eating and aerobic exercise ... This tranquillized

state is normal and healthy. But the compulsive overeater may have become dependent on her own endorphins and the state of food-induced pleasure.[5]

BURYING ANGER

Depression and a sense of loss are often significant with compulsive eaters. Underneath depression there is usually much repressed anger. Compulsive eating can be a 'safe' way to express anger – pushing down food is a means of pushing down feelings. 'The act of overeating provides active, physical release from pent-up anger while allowing the individual to be "nice" and avoid conflict.'[6]

Compulsive eaters may 'feel safer using their mouths to feed themselves than using them to talk and be assertive. They imagine that their fat is making the statement for them while the suffering prevents the words from coming out.'[7] Their weight can become their voice – a way of making quite strong statements about things; a way of saying, 'No', 'I need', 'I want', 'I hate', etc. Losing weight can be like losing their voice.

Doctors at the Minirth-Meier Clinic in Dallas, Texas, make the observation that many of their patients are angry with themselves for something they have done. They punish themselves by overeating then hate themselves for being overweight, which is often less painful than getting in touch with the anger they really feel for the wrong they have done.[8] The difficulty is that, if every time the person feels angry she chooses to react in this way, she never actually learns how to express and handle her anger. Also, holding on to resentment results in a depletion of certain brain chemicals which causes loss of energy and motivation and consequently aids weight gain.

The compulsive eater's weight is also sometimes used by her

as a form of protection to keep other people's anger out. If the sufferer does not like herself, her fat can be seen as the place where all the disliked parts of her are stored. Some women who are very overweight subconsciously protect their self-image by disowning the fat, as if they were saying: 'This is not me – I am the thin person within who has little to do with this enormous figure looking at me from the mirror'.[9]

HIDING FEAR

Sometimes the compulsive eater eats to rebel against the 'perfect image'. She is fed up with trying to live up to the standards which are set. She may feel that she will never attain the 'perfect image' and so she goes to the other extreme of not only abstaining from competing but giving up caring about her body altogether. Some compulsive eaters are actually afraid of being slim. Their fear can be associated with having come to the conclusion that there are certain criteria which go with slimness:

- in control
- happier
- sophisticated
- successful
- respected
- liked
- sexually attractive
- feminine
- wanted

Despite hungering after these criteria, they are concerned that they won't achieve them and so they reason that it's easier not to compete in these things than to risk failing. They may not be aware of needing their fat until they lose it and experience slimness without having worked through the underlying issues. The conclusion can be that being fat feels safer and enables them to cope with life. It also gives them a feeling of strength, compensating for lack of self-worth or confidence. Being slim can mean feeling vulnerable and raw, even cold. The compulsive eater 'is exposed to the very things she attempted to get away from when she got fat in the first place'.[10]

If the very overweight sufferer were to lose significant weight she might also fear being unnoticeable. Her size can cause people to pay attention to her, to hold doors open and to consider her needs. If she were to shrink physically she might disappear from people's view. The thought of being 'a nobody' is painful.

FILLING EMPTINESS

For the compulsive eater, being physically empty can feel terrible because it means that she is likely to get in touch with her deep sense of emotional emptiness. Emptiness feels like death. Often there is also an aching loneliness which other people fail to recognise because the compulsive eater is usually someone who appears to be very involved with people and great fun. The loneliness is not so much through lack of the company of other people, but lack of relating with like-minded people – people who understand her. Pain floods the personality bringing panic that there is nothing able to relieve the terrible ache. Food can easily become a companion at these times.

Many compulsive eaters began eating for comfort or to dispel loneliness as children and have struggled with being overweight since childhood. Overweight children are frequently left out or they win approval by being the joker and funny. 'She's a good laugh,' the other kids might say, but inside the child is feeling isolated or different. As an adult, the more the sufferer is able to allow others to get close, the less she experiences the ache of loneliness, but mentally she often pushes other people away from her, protecting her raw inner self. The compulsive eater is generally someone who takes on a lot and keeps busy. Her inability to say 'No' is both a help and a hindrance to her. It prevents her from thinking too much about how she feels but it also stops her from protecting and looking after herself.

CHAPTER 6

TURNING ROUND

THE PROCESS OF RECOVERY

How do icebergs break up? Put very simply, they melt! However, in the process they can fracture into many pieces. Usually icebergs melt the fastest at the waterline due to the action of waves, but the rate at which they melt and break up depends on water and temperature.[1]

In the same way, eating disorder sufferers go through a process in order that recovery can take place. Within that process, at times, it can feel as though things are getting worse not better, as aspects of the eating disorder fragment and the person feels out of control. Just as with an iceberg, where the abrasive action of the waves begins the melting, so with an eating disorder it is often necessary to hit hard times in order to move on.

Before a sufferer can change, she needs to look at the advantages and disadvantages of having an eating disorder. If there are still too many advantages then change will be impaired. Only *she* can decide when she is ready. Recovery begins with the sufferer admitting that she has a problem and being honest with herself and at least one other person. 'Awareness and compulsion cannot possibly exist together in the same moment. When you turn on a light, it is no longer dark.'[2]

As a person faces her problems, she can feel in two minds about the eating disorder: wanting and yet fearing recovery. It is natural to wonder how she will cope without it. It has been her protection; comfort; guard against feelings; barrier to sexuality; destroyer of loneliness; form of identity and, although sometimes her enemy, also her friend. She has carried it around with her all day, every day – what will she think about if she isn't constantly thinking of food and exercise?

One of the hardest aspects of recovery for the anorexic is to accept weight gain. What if she can't stop eating? Maintaining her weight means losing the sense of achievement which weight loss creates. Bulimics can wonder what would fill the space that bingeing and vomiting has occupied and compulsive eaters may fear that in being thin they will 'disappear'. The fact is that 'Fears about food and eating can only be overcome when the sufferer changes the way she sees herself and develops an optimistic view of her prospects … She cannot enjoy food until she can enjoy life'.[3]

SEEKING HELP

To look at the end goal of full recovery usually sends a sufferer into panic. If she can begin to see that she is not expected to change overnight, and that there are various stages involved in recovery, she will find it far easier to cope.

Even after finding a therapist to whom she can relate, the sufferer can still have mixed feelings. Different defensive reactions are taken into therapy. The anorexic may not admit that she needs much help or she may accept only those parts of the help she wants. She may see receiving help as self-indulgent and could see the therapist as yet another person to avoid upsetting. The bulimic may feel she needs help one week and not the next; equally she may turn up late for an appointment or end up cancelling it at the last minute. She may consider that the therapist, whom she initially thought had all the answers, isn't good enough. The compulsive eater can easily feel that she needs more help than she is getting. She often considers that her problem isn't being solved quickly enough, and fears that the therapist won't be able to cope with her needs.

For recovery to progress, these mixed reactions need to be addressed, and a commitment to working through the eating disorder, most beneficially with someone experienced, needs to be made.

SUPPORT FROM FRIENDS AND FAMILY

In addition to structured therapeutic help with an eating disorder, a support system around the sufferer is of great benefit. However, being a friend to someone who is suffering from an eating disorder is not easy! The friendship invariably goes through a time of testing when the person who is not suffering can lose heart or patience as she watches someone for whom she cares destroying herself. Many people walk away, unable to sustain their commitment.

Most valuable in a friendship is understanding about eating disorders: what it's like to have an eating disorder, how the sufferer is feeling and why she needs this means of coping. Understanding is not merely learning the facts about eating disorders; it's imagining oneself inside the sufferer's skin. What would it be like to feel her feelings, have her fears and see the world through her eyes? The choice of words and comments is important. An anorexic or bulimic will find comments about a change in weight difficult and such comments may reinforce her determination to take control of her body. 'You look your old self again' can be frightening if the sufferer hated herself before the illness. It is more helpful to focus on overall change and efforts towards recovery, rather than simply weight.

> While encouraging the sufferer to become more expressive and more accurately aware of how she currently is, it is crucial for the helper to remain tuned to the fact that the sufferer's real self is so tentative and fragile she does not have the resources to cope with even the most minor intrusions. Even talking to her can leave her feeling invaded, exploited, controlled. So it must be made equally clear to her that it is entirely acceptable for her to keep her thoughts, feelings and experiences to herself. She does not have to share them with the helper, and it is important that the helper does not create an obligation, unspoken or otherwise, that she should.[4]

Support from family is more complex than friends, in that some of the interactions between the parents and sufferer will have been feeding the eating disorder. The family may feel shocked that their child has an eating disorder or grieved over how their family seems to have 'fallen apart' since their child became ill. But blaming oneself or the sufferer will not resolve the situation. It is more constructive to look at what changes need to be made. Many parents coping with a child who has an eating disorder feel angry. Parents have a right to their feelings, but it is important to separate the behaviour of the sufferer from the person, and hence feel angry with the eating disorder rather than individual.

Care should be taken not to punish the sufferer for being ill – the distortions in the sufferer's thinking, her lack of communication, irritability and defensive reactions can be due partly to malnutrition. Parents need to be firm but consistently loving. One of the most beneficial things a family can do for a sufferer is to understand what she is trying to communicate through the eating disorder.

As the sufferer faces her eating disorder, a necessary part of the recovery process is taking responsibility for herself, appropriate to her age. It is better to encourage her to take responsibility and support her as she struggles to do so than to step in and rescue her. The exception is if she's becoming seriously ill physically and needs to be hospitalised. It is important not to shield the child from pain, disappointment or growing up, and not to overprotect her.

A crucial struggle is for parents and children to separate with love. The relationship of parent and child has to be severed and then slowly soothed and healed into something new. As long as parents feel overly responsible for their child, the child will not grow up and face life on its own. The separation is not just a matter of age or geographics. It is a deep emotional commitment and tie which must be broken for survival to occur.[5]

The relationship between a sufferer and partner, parent, friend or helper needs to be one that empowers and fosters an environment which is conducive to change. One concept which is helpful is to access interactions in terms of Transactional Analysis. Put very simply, we all have within us the ability to relate as an adult, a nurturing parent, a critical parent, a free child or a hurt child. Healthy relating between two grown people is adult to adult. If the sufferer is relating in 'hurt child' mode then it is easy for the other person to fall into nurturing or critical parent. Adult to adult relating empowers and enables the sufferer to take responsibility which is a key to recovery.

SEEKING FULL RECOVERY

Thinking again of icebergs, one frequently asked question about icebergs is, 'Do they hit the bottom?' They certainly do! Icebergs often 'ground', 'hit the seabed' and 'get stuck'. This commonly happens along the coast where icebergs are brought into shore by irregular tidal currents or strong winds. Sometimes icebergs 'scour' the seabed resulting in irregular troughs several kilometers in length being created.[6]

In the same way, it is common for eating disorders to both 'hit the bottom' and to 'ground'; for sufferers to become 'stuck' in their recovery. Figures showing the percentage of people who recover vary. Both short-term and long-term studies of patients with anorexia indicate that full recovery occurs in fewer than 50 per cent of the patients studied.[7] Calculating the average outcome in nine representative studies, it was shown that 22 per cent of patients with anorexia, most of whom had been hospitalised, remained chronically ill or had a poor outcome; 8 per cent died. These figures were derived from a follow-up averaging ten years.[8] Comparable studies have not yet been conducted for bulimia or compulsive eating, but poor outcome is also known to be common.

Full recovery is possible for every sufferer. Sadly, many do not find it because they receive unhelpful, inadequate or insufficient treatment; are not motivated to change; are trapped in circumstances which perpetuate the problem; or do not have the necessary support. One of the other major stumbling blocks to recovery is that there is nearly always a pay-off to having an eating disorder. This isn't unique to eating disorders! Jesus, at times, asked, 'Do you want to get well?' With eating disorders the pay-off can be: lower expectations from others; people asking how she is; not facing the adult world … and much more!

For recovery to happen, it is important that all components are addressed. We are physical, emotional and spiritual beings, and with eating disorders there is brokenness in all three areas. The different areas include:

- Physical: food, weight, nutrition
- Emotional: feelings, thoughts, reactions, behaviours and choices
- Spiritual: freedom, identity, maturity

In the remaining chapters of the book, each of these areas is going to be looked at in further detail. But firstly it can be helpful to look at what recovery is so that it is clear what the aim is.

ATTAINING RECOVERY

When thinking about recovery, it can be difficult to know where to begin! A friend of mine, Kim, who suffered the whole spectrum of eating disorders, said that she only really made progress in recovery when she took specific action. The starting point for her was a prayer. 'Lord, I'm willing for you to do *anything* in my life in order for me to get well.' She was willing to give up the most important things to her, work as a professional actress and the importance of body image, in order to recover. She'd tried everything in her own power to get well and it hadn't worked and she came to the conclusion that she was never going to be free unless she chose to let go of the control, submit the eating disorder to God and make getting over her eating disorder a *priority*. From that point onwards things changed! In her own journey she said the following were essential to her recovery:

1. Making the decision to get better.
2. Working out a viable strategy.
3. Reaching out for help.
4. Modifying her circumstances.
5. Building in emotional and spiritual support.
6. Facing the pain.
7. Developing trust and allowing time.

These concepts are expounded in 'New ID', a course for people struggling with eating disorders.[9]

Recovery from an eating disorder is far more than just appearing 'normal' in weight and eating and includes:

1. A healthy weight, ie one that is not excessively under or over that which is considered appropriate for the person's height and age – 10 per cent within average is a suggestion.
2. A life which is no longer centred on food and weight and where eating is not a response merely to controlling calories or weight fluctuations.
3. Flexibility in eating and the ability to eat three meals a day without guilt; and the ability to occasionally overeat or skip a meal without being tempted to starve, binge or vomit.

4. The return of all disturbed bodily functions, such as menstruation.
5. The ability to express and process emotions (well or not so well) without using food as a means of coping.
6. A move away from 'thinking errors' tied in with the eating disorder, such as 'black and white thinking'. (See chapter 9.)
7. The freedom to act out of choice, not duty, and to make choices as a person separate from food and weight or the persuasions of others.
8. A move away from eating disorder patterns mirrored in relationships, eg letting go of withdrawal and control for the anorexic, push-pull relating for the bulimic and the need to consume for the compulsive eater.
9. The establishing of two-way adult relationships. The ability to live in the adult world and conduct life accordingly, such as hold down a job and take responsibility.
10. Emotional and physical separation from parents, appropriate to the person's age, and the establishing of a separate identity.
11. The ability to have fun and integrate different aspects of life into everyday living as opposed to life being controlled by the requirements of the eating disorder.
12. Not exchanging the eating disorder for another addiction.

CHAPTER 7

FACING REALITY

DECIDING TO CHANGE

If a ship is heading towards an iceberg, it has to recognise the danger, face the reality of the situation and decide on a course of action. Likewise, with an eating disorder, there comes a point at which it is necessary to face the reality of what is happening to the body and the destructiveness of the eating patterns, and a conscious decision has to be made to work on dietary changes.

PHYSICAL: BODY AND NUTRITION

Eating disorders are addictions and unlike many addictions where the person can choose to abstain from the addictive product for the rest of his/her life, food has to be faced and consumed every day! Hence it cannot be cut out, as can, for example, alcohol – it must be changed!

Overcoming an eating disorder does not just involve gaining weight if anorexic, losing weight if a compulsive eater or no longer bingeing and vomiting if bulimic. Rather, it is about establishing a *healthy relationship* with food and a *realistic attitude* towards one's body. The goal for the compulsive eater should be not slimness but to stop using food as a means of masking problems, giving comfort, burying feelings and filling emptiness. The goal for the anorexic and bulimic should not be weight gain and no longer bingeing or compensating for what has been eaten, but freedom in relationship with food.

Heckel points out that an overeater cannot be considered cured, even if she loses weight, unless the other symptoms have cleared up. The result will be 'thin fat people';[1] people who may now be thin but are still fat in their mentality. Equally, if anorexics and bulimics change their eating patterns but still hold onto distorted beliefs concerning food and weight, then they remain anorexic/bulimic in their mentality.

In terms of recovery for all eating disorders there needs to be a change in a) attitude and, b) eating patterns. Without significant change in both areas, and the underlying issues being dealt with, the person is susceptible to relapse.

A) ATTITUDE

The changes which need to take place in terms of attitude tend to be in the areas of:

1. The function of food
2. Dieting mentality
3. Lack of beginnings and endings

1. THE FUNCTION OF FOOD

The original function of food is to provide the body with fuel (energy), and by eating the right balance of nutrients, to help the body function well. However, in the Western culture we have complicated the role of food by mixing food with emotions and giving it specific labels such as 'good' and 'bad'; 'naughty' and 'nice'. Once we label food 'good' or 'bad' we then label ourselves 'good' or 'bad' according to what we have eaten.

In addition, there are two further complications in our relationship with food: we interpret emotional hunger as physical hunger, and we spend our lives concentrating on calorific rather than nutritional values. To attain freedom from food having a hold over a person, it is necessary for there to be a clear distinction between the responses to physical and emotional hunger. A change is also needed in the way food is perceived, concentrating on its usefulness to our functioning rather than its effect on body image.

2. DIETING MENTALITY

Another stumbling block in recovery is that because food is categorised 'good' and 'bad' (sometimes known as 'naughty'), a whole mindset is developed which is geared towards avoiding certain foods. Everyone has their own classification of 'bad foods' but on the whole it tends to be those that result in weight gain. When we avoid foods because we tell ourselves we are bad if we want them or have them, then we end up craving them! If, however, the same food types are avoided for reasons other than a diet mentality, it doesn't usually result in the same cravings! Food is not 'good' or 'bad'; some foods are more useful to our bodies than others – some food types are required in greater amounts and others are required in less amounts.

Recovery involves the sufferer letting go of dieting and letting go of the war within herself over food. 'War requires at least two sides. When you decide that you will listen to yourself and not to your calorie-counter or your fears, there is nothing to rebel against. There is nothing you can't have tomorrow so there is no reason to eat it all today'.[2] At first it is hard for the sufferer not to count the calories in every mouthful. A conscious decision to see food as nourishment, not fat, needs to be made. As life becomes filled with greater meaning, and underlying causes are dealt with, eating disorders cease to serve a purpose and counting calories begins to diminish.

3. LACK OF BEGINNINGS AND ENDINGS

Again, because of the 'dieting' mentality the sufferer fails to give herself sufficient quantities of the right balance of foods and fails to establish a clear beginning and ending to her eating. Shirley Billigmeier, in her book *Inner Eating*,[3] talks about the eating act. She says that each time we eat we begin a new eating act, like a circle. Our circle needs a beginning and an ending and should contain all we need to sustain us to the next eating act. Ideally we should have three circles a day, but if we do not have the correct amount and balance within a circle we can easily end up with a mass of little circles which merge into each other, known as chaotic eating! She points out that by putting a beginning and an ending to our eating we

- own what we are eating
- can see clearly the amounts and how often we are eating
- give ourselves the freedom to think about things other than food
- clarify our internal boundaries

If we do not set healthy boundaries in eating then

- we are likely to look for external boundaries (diet) which are set by someone else
- we respond to food with hidden messages which ruin our choices
- our eating is governed by our feelings, rather than what our body needs
- food ends up ruling our life and dominating our thinking

B) EATING PATTERNS

Without working on attitude, any attempt to sustain healthy eating patterns is likely to fail, hence it is essential to work with both attitude and eating patterns. Because of the 'dieting mentality', our concept of 'healthy' is not always accurate. The 'healthy' diet held by many people with eating disorders is geared around calorific value and low fat. In April 2005, the USDA released its interactive dietary guidelines. A new food pyramid replaced the old four basic food groups. In the new pyramid, plant oils, nuts and seeds feature more notably, as seen in Fig 1.[4] The new pyramid is not dissimilar to the Mediterranean foods pyramid, where olive oil plays a significant part in the diet, as seen in Fig 2.[5]

Another factor involved in healthy eating is the Glycemic Index which ranks foods from 0 to 100 according to the effect on blood sugar levels after eating. GI, as it is known, was developed in 1981 by David Jenkins and Thomas Wolever of the University of Toronto for diabetes but is very helpful for stabilising eating patterns and weight. When we eat foods that have high-GI numbers, we feel an initial boost in energy and blood sugar rises, but this is followed by a cycle of increased fat storage, sluggishness, and greater hunger. Low-GI foods (less than 55) produce a gradual rise in blood sugar that releases energy slowly and do not cause sudden highs and lows in energy and mood.[6]

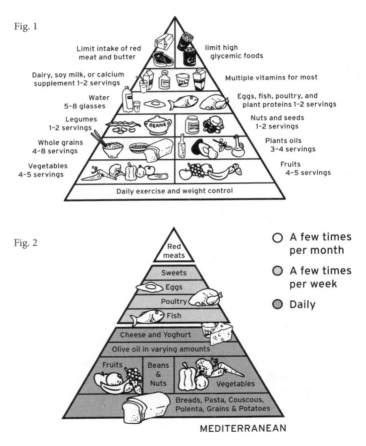

Fig. 1

Limit intake of red meat and butter
limit high glycemic foods
Dairy, soy milk, or calcium supplement 1-2 servings
Multiple vitamins for most
Water 5-8 glasses
Eggs, fish, poultry, and plant proteins 1-2 servings
Legumes 1-2 servings
Nuts and seeds 1-2 servings
Whole grains 4-8 servings
Plants oils 3-4 servings
Vegetables 4-5 servings
Fruits 4-5 servings
Daily exercise and weight control

Fig. 2

Red meats
Sweets
Eggs
Poultry
Fish
Cheese and Yoghurt
Olive oil in varying amounts
Fruits
Beans & Nuts
Vegetables
Breads, Pasta, Couscous, Polenta, Grains & Potatoes

○ A few times per month
◐ A few times per week
● Daily

MEDITERRANEAN

HELP FROM A NUTRITIONIST

In order to implement changes in attitude towards food and weight, counselling/therapy can be helpful; in order to implement changes in eating patterns, seeing a nutritionist can be helpful. As well as advice on dietary changes for weight gain or weight loss, a nutritionist can detect vitamin and mineral deficiencies, food intolerances and other factors which can complicate recovery from an eating disorder.

Where it is not possible to see a nutritionist, the following simple guidelines are worth considering:

1. Aim to eat three meals a day, including breakfast. Breakfast is important as it stabilises blood sugar levels and helps to prevent a later binge. (If eating first thing in the morning is really too difficult then for a period of time, try a late breakfast.)
2. Where possible, always eat wholegrain products (such as brown rice, brown pasta, wholemeal bread, quinoa) and avoid processed food (such as white flour and white sugar. A lot of artificial sweetener is also not helpful).
3. Set in place a beginning and an ending to eating. Within each 'eating act' establish what the body really requires for functioning rather than what your mind is telling you you are 'allowed' to eat.
4. Drink plenty of water and keep caffeine levels to a minimum. Consider alternative drinks such as Rooibos tea.
5. In your mind, separate plant oils and essential fatty acids from 'fat'. Our bodies need these oils for healthy functioning. A deficiency can lead to infections and a weakening of the immune system. Include oil, such as olive oil, in your daily

diet. It lowers cholesterol!

6. Where weight gain is needed, introduce snacks *between* meals rather than increasing the meal portion itself. When weight has been achieved this means that extra food can easily be withdrawn without altering meals. For snacks consider nuts, dried fruit, grapes, milk.

7. Consider taking a multi-vitamin/mineral supplement and an EFA supplement with food daily. Digestive enzymes and a probiotic formula can also be helpful.

8. Avoid nibbling at food when preparing meals or eating leftovers. This would be considered outside the eating boundaries and can easily lead to chaotic eating.

9. Make the conscious choice not to weigh yourself every day. The slightest fluctuation can result in the desire to take drastic action or to feel disillusioned. Having an external source of accountability regarding weight can be helpful.

10. Take moderate exercise but try not to attach this to eating. Where weight gain is necessary, exercise will need to be limited; equally, where weight loss is needed, exercise will need to be increased.

11. Endeavour not to go shopping when hungry as the risk of buying binge foods might increase. Buy in only what is needed in the next day or two and, where possible, do not keep in the house foods which are high risk for binges.

12. Eat at a table and remind yourself that food is available tomorrow.

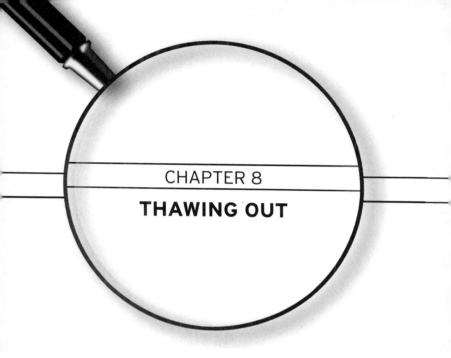

CHAPTER 8

THAWING OUT

FACING THE FEELINGS

In chapter 6, we asked the question, 'How do icebergs break up?', and discovered that, basically, they melt. However, in the process they often calve and fracture into many pieces. For the eating disorder sufferer, work has to take place at an emotional level which is not dissimilar! Getting in touch with emotions and working through past pain is essential for healing and freedom, and can be a bit like thawing which, at times, can feel messy.

The sufferer needs to recognise different feelings when they arise, to find new ways of coping. Each of the eating disorders will have served its purpose in relation to emotions and trauma:

Anorexia: numbing all feelings; denying needs; locking away trauma.

Bulimia: splitting off negative feelings; admitting needs, but not being able to hold onto them; pushing trauma away.
Compulsive eating: pushing feelings down; swallowing needs in fear that they won't be met; submerging trauma.

The sufferer will need to:
- Gain an accurate understanding of the role that emotions play in life.
- Develop means of dealing with emotions and trauma outside of addictive and self-destructive patterns.
- Address the roots of persistent and repetitive negative emotions.

GAIN AN ACCURATE UNDERSTANDING OF THE ROLE THAT EMOTIONS PLAY IN LIFE

The sufferer has a tendency to judge her emotions: 'I shouldn't feel this way because …', 'Feeling angry is bad.' If she wants to make progress, she needs to change the way feelings are viewed. Feelings are not 'good' or 'bad', only 'comfortable' or 'uncomfortable'. She must discover that it's OK to admit vulnerability, cry, feel sad, feel angry or disagree, as long as these feelings can be expressed in a way which does not intentionally hurt her or anyone else. All feelings need to be acknowledged and valued as a part of the person. 'Getting to know your feelings is part of getting to know yourself as a unique person'[1] but most sufferers struggle to know how they feel and tend to see negative emotions as threatening, leaving them feeling powerless to handle them.

Whilst doing part of my counselling training at CWR, I found the teaching given by Selwyn Hughes on the relationship between emotions and goals of enormous benefit and have often used this concept with sufferers.

Emotions can be put into three main groups, each of which has a goal:

1. Guilt = unreachable goal
2. Anxiety = uncertain goal
3. Anger = blocked goal

For instance, if an anorexic set herself the goal of only eating 100 calories a day, which due to others watching her eating was unreachable, and she ended up eating 600, she would feel guilty. If she set the goal of needing to know every ingredient in what she ate, then going for a meal would result in an uncertain goal and she would feel anxious. If she set the goal of preparing her own food and then someone else blocked that goal by preparing the food, she would feel angry.

These are all quite simple explanations of how goals relate specifically to food and weight issues for an anorexic, but equally the principle can be related to many different situations in people's lives. Understanding what is behind an emotion is one of the keys to overcoming the feeling of powerlessness. When we understand what's going on, we have the choice and ability to work on overwhelming emotions.

DEVELOP MEANS OF DEALING WITH EMOTIONS AND TRAUMA OUTSIDE OF ADDICTIVE AND SELF-DESTRUCTIVE PATTERNS

It is important for a sufferer to be helped to realise that her eating disorder is an unhealthy and destructive way of dealing with emotions. Throughout most of the time of having the eating disorder she will, consciously or subconsciously, have been responding to negative emotions through food and weight. Her eating patterns are a form of communicating how she feels and a means of destroying her emotions and/or not facing the reality of them.

Developing different means of dealing with emotions outside of addictive and self-destructive patterns will involve recognising how entwined food patterns and emotions have become, and separating the two. A variety of ways can be used to help the sufferer to express her emotions and gain insight into what's going on. The following are a few examples of creative tools which use a different part of the brain and enable a person to access emotions more easily:

1. Therapeutic art
2. Clay work
3. Dolls and toys
4. Drama
5. Lists of words
6. Pictures and illustrations
7. Observing the body
8. Writing

Just talking about hurts does not necessarily release the pain; the sufferer actually needs to *feel* and express her emotions. There are three levels of expression of feelings. The first is to notice and acknowledge what is going on. The second is verbal expression: 'I feel hurt.' The third involves the physical release of feelings – through tears, shouting or trembling.[2]

Becoming more confident with emotions is paramount to recovery. The more a sufferer allows herself to feel her feelings, the less scary it becomes to have them. But feeling alone is not adequate; however, it is necessary to process emotions. Many people struggle to know how to do this and hence during teaching courses on overcoming eating disorders, I put together what I call 'Seven Strategies for Processing Emotions':

1. Identify the emotion (give it a name, eg guilt, anger).
2. Acknowledge that's how you feel (remember to *own* the emotion, 'I feel ...').
3. Understand why it is there (is your goal unreachable, uncertain, blocked ... why?).
4. Express it
   a) emotionally (rationalise it in your head and talk with someone who can be objective)
   b) spiritually (talk to God and gain His perspective using Scripture, eg the Psalms)
5. Look at your options of dealing with it: (eg one situation I had to deal with when renovating a charity property involved a builder who had promised to remove a wall, opening up two rooms into one in time for me to run a teaching day. Two days before the event, the job had not been done and I felt angry – blocked goal. My goal was for there to be space for the people to enjoy the day!)
   a) assertive (eg insist the builder does the job, even if only the day before!)
   b) practical (eg move the event to the church up the road)
   c) defeatist (eg cancel the event)
   d) apologist (eg pack people into the one room and apologise for the squeeze!)
   e) independent (eg knock the wall down myself!)

6. Decide on which action you will take. (Choosing to take action brings about greater resolution to your emotions than simply stopping at the point of expressing your feelings!)
7. Leave it there! (Once you have made your choice over what to do, stick with it!)

We all have a tendency to think that we have dealt with our emotions when we reach the point of expression. But I have a theory that unless we look at options for dealing with the emotion and make a decision on consequent action, we don't actually process our emotions, we just feel them. To process emotions is to be empowered!

If at the end of step seven the emotion is still particularly troublesome, it may be necessary to go back to the beginning of the list and complete the process again!

ADDRESS THE ROOTS OF PERSISTENT AND REPETITIVE NEGATIVE EMOTIONS

When we consider the whole picture of an iceberg, we realise that there is far more to it than meets the eye. In the same way, how we experience our emotions *now* is affected by unprocessed emotions from the *past*. Colin A. Ross, author of 'The Trauma Model' and founder of The Ross Institute, Richardson, Dallas, Texas[3], also uses the 'Spectrum of Emotions' in his treatment programmes. It was devised by Melissa Caldwell, MS, LPC, ATR, Executive Clinical Director of The Ross Institute.

The chart below explains in part the 'Spectrum of Emotions'. People without past trauma operate in what is known as the Grounded-Present. They experience a whole range of emotions and these emotions fit the situations they are currently facing.

People with a traumatic history often do not operate in the Grounded-Present but instead their emotions are fuelled by previously painful situations and hence they operate from the position of Ungrounded-Past. Their emotions are experienced as extremes, such as: Numb or Terror/Panic; Numb or Despair/Hopelessness.

For instance, if someone who operates in the Grounded-Present is let down by a friend not turning up to give them a lift, they might feel hurt or angry. In contrast, someone who operates in the Ungrounded-Past might feel numbness, despair or rage.

UNGROUNDED-PAST EXTREME	GROUNDED-PRESENT BALANCED	UNGROUNDED-PAST EXTREME
Numb	Afraid/Fear	Terror/Panic
Numb	Hurt	Despair/Hopelessness
Numb	Anger	Rage

Colin Ross lists many different emotions, numbness being a viable alternative to extreme emotional reactions. In order to dilute an extreme emotional reaction as a form of graded exposure programme for emotional experiences, it is suggested that by using a see-saw type idea and placing rage on one end and sadness on the other, one could slide from one emotional state to the other without becoming overwhelmed. The 'window' of tolerance in the Grounded-Present grows through experience and time.

In helping a person to know if what they are experiencing is outside the normal 'balanced' area, it is useful to ask: 'Does the situation justify the intensity of the emotion being felt?' If the answer is 'No', then it's likely to be fuelled by the past, and is therefore creating what is known as a 'mismatch' between emotional responses and what's happening in the present.

Healing involves making sense of situations from the past that have fuelled extreme emotions, and learning to operate in the Grounded-Present. It also involves learning a whole new way of coping with the stresses that life brings and working through any past issues and damage. Unless these areas are dealt with it can be that the sufferer recovers from an eating disorder in terms of eating but remains an anorexic, bulimic or compulsive eater at an emotional and relational level. Alternatively, it may be that she goes on to develop another addictive pattern, unhealthy coping strategy or disorder.

People who have not faced their pain often repeat with others the very behaviour patterns which have hurt them; or re-enact their past in other relationships, hoping to change the ending to a happier outcome. It is useful to be aware of possible triggers which send a sufferer into these patterns. Many behaviours are developed to escape the reality of how painful life is, but as someone once said: 'If only we realised that the indirect way we choose in order to avoid pain is just as painful as the pain we try so skillfully to avoid ...'[4]

Dealing with overwhelming emotional experiences will bring far greater self-acceptance for the sufferer. Dag Hammarskjöld said: 'A man who is at war with himself will be at war with others.'[5] The sufferer rarely feels that she has a choice with her emotions, but she does. The more she has explored the purpose that her eating disorder serves and worked through childhood hurts, the greater her awareness of choice. Victor Frankl, a psychiatrist, makes the point that we are choosing beings. We can't always choose our circumstances, but we can always choose our responses.[6]

CHAPTER 9

CHANGING VIEWS

SHAPED BY THOUGHTS

In looking at an iceberg, people can gasp with horror and declare that their ship will sink, or they can talk through the options for dealing with the situation. Similarly, the thinking behind an eating disorder controls the future happiness, freedom and potential of the individual.

It is essential for thinking to change in order for recovery from an eating disorder both to be possible and sustainable. The Bible says: 'Be careful how you think; your life is shaped by your thoughts' (Prov. 4:23, GNB). How the sufferer thinks affects the way she feels and the choices she makes.

Albert Ellis, a clinical psychologist, developed what he terms The 'ABC Theory of Emotion':[1]

A = the activating event
B = the belief system
C = the consequent emotion

His point is that it is not the event in itself which results in the emotion, but rather what the person believes or says about the event. For instance, if someone you know walks straight past you, you can feel hurt. Why? Because you may be saying to yourself, 'I'm not important' or 'She purposely didn't say hello'. If, instead, your response was, 'She's obviously in a hurry or didn't see me' then you would not feel hurt and rejected.

DESTRUCTIVE MESSAGES

Whilst it is important for change to take place in several aspects of the sufferer's life, one of the key areas will involve working on the faulty belief system, not just in terms of how she perceives food and weight but how she interprets different situations in everyday life. Faulty thinking arises out of messages received as a child which are further developed and distorted as an adult. Words spoken repeatedly by a child's parents, teachers, school friends or her own interpretations, can influence quite dramatically the way a child views herself and her world:

- 'You never do anything right'
- 'I can't trust you'
- 'You're bad/wicked'
- 'What will the neighbours think?'
- 'You don't belong in our group'
- 'Fatty; sausage legs; moon-face; ugly features'
- 'You ought to do better/have known better'
- 'People won't like you if you cry'

SELF-TALK

As a child, by frequently hearing destructive and negative words about herself, the potential sufferer will eventually begin to behave as though they are true and develop a distorted picture of herself. 'You don't belong in our group' she might translate into 'I'm not liked'. This can cause the person to withdraw from others, which in turn means that others give up approaching her, which then re-enforces her belief that she's not liked. She concludes: 'I'm different, a failure and bad.' Her self-worth and self-confidence drop lower by the day.

Messages received which are taken on board and then repeated internally are known as self-talk. It is said that we speak to ourselves at a rate of 1,300 words per minute.[2] If most of those words are self-condemnatory, no wonder the sufferer walks around in a perpetual state of feeling as though she is stuck at the bottom of a pit full of thick mud!

Albert Ellis and his colleagues identified ten common irrational beliefs which, if held too rigidly, are likely to lead to emotional distress. These beliefs are learned early in life and become the bedrock from which our thinking patterns spring.[3]

1. I must be liked or accepted by every important person in my life, for almost everything I do.
2. I must be successful, competent and achieving in everything I do if I'm to consider myself worthwhile.
3. It is awful and terrible when things are not the way I would like them to be. Things should be different.
4. I must feel anxious, upset and preoccupied if something is, or may be, dangerous.
5. Human unhappiness is caused by events beyond our control so people have little or no ability to control their negative feelings.

6. It is easier to avoid facing many of life's difficulties and responsibilities than to face them.
7. The past is all-important, so if something once strongly affected one's life, it cannot be altered.
8. When people act badly, inadequately or unfairly, I blame them, and view them as completely bad or pathetic – including myself.
9. Maximum happiness can be achieved by inertia and inaction, or by passively enjoying oneself.
10. Everyone should be dependent on others and I need someone stronger than myself on whom I can rely.

In addition to looking at this list of ten beliefs, it is helpful for the sufferer to make a list of regular self-talk relating to: a) the eating disorder, and b) herself.

A) THE EATING DISORDER
- 'I can't change'
- 'Being thin means everything will be OK'
- 'If I could just lose weight I'd feel different'
- 'I'll never stop putting on weight'
- 'I can't go out for a meal if I can't be sick afterwards'
- 'I have to take laxatives otherwise …'
- 'No one understands'

B) HERSELF
- 'I must never be wrong'
- 'I should think only "proper" thoughts'
- 'What I want doesn't count'
- 'I'm stupid'

- 'I could and ought to do better'
- 'I should always be strong'
- 'I should never upset other people'
- 'If people really cared they would know what I need'
- 'People don't like me'
- 'To be accepted I have to be how others want me to be'
- 'When someone is angry with me it's my fault'
- 'If I don't do what people want then they won't like me'
- 'I must always make other people happy'

Research has highlighted particular types of 'thinking errors' and it can be helpful to try and identify self-talk related to these.[4]

- **All-or-nothing thinking.** You think in absolutes, as either black or white, good or bad, with no middle ground. You tend to judge people or events using general labels, for example 'he's an idiot', 'I'm hopeless', 'I'll never learn to drive', 'I'm a complete failure'. You may condemn yourself completely as a person on the basis of a single event.
- **Awfulising – catastrophising.** You tend to magnify and exaggerate the importance of events and how awful or unpleasant they will be, over-estimating the chances of disaster; whatever can go wrong will go wrong. If you have a setback you will view it as a never-ending pattern of defeat.
- **Personalising.** You take responsibility and blame for anything unpleasant even if it has little or nothing to do with you. If something bad happens you immediately think 'it's my fault'.
- **Negative focus.** You focus on the negative, ignoring or misinterpreting positive aspects of a situation. You focus on your weaknesses and forget your strengths, looking on the

dark side. If you've done a good job, you filter out and reject the positive comments and focus on the negative.

- **Jumping to conclusions.** You make negative interpretations even though there are no definite facts. You start predicting the future, and take on the mantle of 'mind reader'. You are likely to predict that negative things will happen.
- **Living by fixed rules.** You tend to have fixed rules and unrealistic expectations, regularly using the words 'should', 'ought', 'must' and 'can't'. This leads to unnecessary guilt and disappointment. The more rigid these statements are, the more disappointed, angry, depressed or guilty you are likely to feel.

'Exaggerated thoughts' and 'black and white thinking' are examples of 'all-or-nothing thinking', and the following may help you to know how to expand on the different thinking errors and relate them to eating disorders.

EXAGGERATED THOUGHTS
- 'People being angry or criticising me is intolerable'
- 'It's disastrous when things go wrong'
- 'If I'm in pain it's unbearable not to have relief straight away'
- 'Being fat's the worst thing in the world'

BLACK AND WHITE THINKING
- 'If I eat this biscuit I'll get fat'
- 'If I don't starve I'll never stop eating'
- 'If I don't get all A grades I'm a failure'
- 'If I'm not liked by everyone I must be hated by everyone'

CORRECTING THINKING

As thoughts arise, or having asked herself what thoughts lie behind her negative feelings, the sufferer then needs to challenge the thinking and apply truth, eg:

Thought 'I should never upset other people'
Challenge 'Am I responsible for other people's feelings?'
Truth 'I can't avoid accidentally upsetting others sometimes and I am not responsible for their feelings or reactions.'
Thought 'If people really cared they would know what I need'
Challenge 'Is it fair to expect other people to guess what I need?'
Truth 'Just because a person doesn't guess what I need doesn't mean they don't care. It's unreasonable to expect them to guess, and it's up to me to ask.'

There are certain questions which a person can ask to help them consider whether thoughts are causing problems, such as:

- Am I thinking in all-or-nothing terms?
- Am I condemning myself as a total person on the basis of a single event?
- Am I concentrating on my weaknesses and forgetting my strengths?
- Am I blaming myself for something which is not my fault?
- Am I taking something personally which has little or nothing to do with me?
- Am I expecting myself to be perfect?
- Am I using a double standard – how would I view someone else in my situation?

- Am I paying attention only to the black side of things?
- Am I overestimating the chances of disaster?
- Am I exaggerating the importance of events?
- Am I fretting about the way things ought to be instead of accepting and dealing with them as they come?
- Am I assuming I can do nothing to change my situation?
- Am I predicting the future instead of experimenting with it?[5]

What has to take place for the sufferer is a renewing of her mind. The Bible tells us: 'Do not conform any longer to the pattern of this world, but be transformed by the renewing of your mind' (Rom. 12:2). J.B. Phillips translates the same verse: 'Don't let the world around you squeeze you into its own mould, but let God remake you so that your whole attitude of mind is changed ...'

CHAPTER 10

BREAKING FREE

LOOSENING THE HOLD

When an iceberg has dominated the horizon and posed no end of danger to passing ships, it must be awesome to see it eventually disappear! The same is true with an eating disorder!

In chapter 6 we spoke of how icebergs often 'ground' and 'scour' the seabed. I believe, that with an eating disorder, part of the 'being grounded' and 'scouring the seabed' is spiritual and therefore requires a spiritual answer.

In the New Testament, the book of Romans paints a good picture of the contrast between 'being stuck' and 'being free', and *what* makes the difference, or rather *who* makes the difference!

In particular, Romans 7 talks about the person who is locked into unhelpful patterns and who has an instinctive knowledge about what is right, but who can't live it. 'For I joyfully concur with the law of God in the inner man, but I see a different law in the members of my body, waging war against the law of my mind, and making me a prisoner of the law of sin which is in my members' (Rom. 7:22–23, NASB). Eating disorders are so similar! In essence, people with eating disorders know what they need to do but they can't do it; they can't get out of the addictive behaviour cycle they are in.

Romans 8 talks about the person who is free, who has no guilt or shame before God, and who knows his/her identity as God's child. It is indicative of a life without an eating disorder!

A friend of mine, Kim, who created 'New ID', a course for people struggling with eating disorders, asks the question, 'How do we get out of Romans 7 and into Romans 8?' She points out that it is a journey and that we need a starting point on that journey. For both of us, the starting point was Jesus. In Romans 7:24, Paul asks, 'Wretched man that I am! Who will set me free from the body of this death?' (NASB). He replies: 'Thanks be to God through Jesus Christ our Lord!' (Rom. 7:25, NASB). The New Testament meaning of 'set me free' is 'to deliver or to draw out of danger or calamity and to liberate'. That is what God wants to do for the eating disorder sufferer; to draw her out of danger and to liberate her, and the Person who can do that, as Paul says, is Jesus!

Paul goes on to say, 'Therefore there is now no condemnation for those who are in Christ Jesus. For the law of the Spirit of life in Christ Jesus has set you free from the law of sin and death. For what the Law could not do, weak as it was through the flesh, God did …' (Rom 8:1–3, NASB). Overcoming an eating disorder involves much work from the sufferer and much help from outside, but I believe there is also a part of the sufferer's freedom that comes only from God!

THE SPIRITUAL HOLD

Essentially, eating disorders are addictions and addictions are strongholds from which only God can bring release. A stronghold is something that has a strong hold over you. The dictionary defines 'stronghold' as, 'a fortress, a place of security, a refuge', and this is the role that the eating disorder plays. However, the safe place soon becomes a prison in which the sufferer is locked. The will alone is not sufficient to break a stronghold. 'For our struggle is not against flesh and blood, but against the rulers, against the authorities, against the powers of this dark world and against the spiritual forces of evil in the heavenly realms' (Eph. 6:12).

> Fortresses (or 'strongholds' in the King James Version) are fleshly thought patterns that were programmed into your mind when you learned to live your life independently of God. Your worldview was shaped by the environment you were raised in. But when you became a Christian, nobody pressed the 'CLEAR' button. Your old fleshly habit patterns of thought weren't erased.
>
> What was learned has to be unlearned. If you have trained wrong, can you be retrained? If you believed a lie, can you renounce that lie and believe the truth? Can your mind be reprogrammed? That is what repentance is: a change of mind. We are transformed by the renewing of our minds because we have the mind of Christ within us and because the Holy Spirit will lead us into all truth. But the world system we were raised in and our independent flesh patterns are not the only enemies of our sanctification ... we still battle the world, the flesh and the devil.[1]

It makes sense that the sufferer needs to renounce thoughts and actions which have set themselves up against the truth. It is also important that areas of the sufferer's life where the enemy has attacked are prayed through. Equally significant in the process of recovery is the sufferer's choice to let go of the control of her life, which needs to be handed back to God.

LETTING GO

What the sufferer needs to let go of is the control that the eating disorder has had and the identity that it has given her. For many people these are the hardest aspects of recovery.

Letting go of control requires surrender. The dictionary definition of surrender is to 'relinquish possession or control'; to surrender to God means that we become fully His, and not our own.

> Even though we pray about our challenges and problems, all too often what we really want is strength to accomplish what we've already decided is best for ourselves and others. Meanwhile we press on with our own priorities and plans. We remain the scriptwriter, casting director, choreographer and producer of the drama of our own lives, in which we are the star performer.[2]

HONESTY, REPENTANCE, BOLD LOVE AND FORGIVENESS

Honesty, repentance and bold love are also part of the letting go of the old and embracing the new.

> Honesty removes the pleasant, antiseptic blandness of denial. Repentance strips away self-contempt and other-centred hatred and replaces it with humility, grief and tenderness. Bold love increases power and freedom through the exhilaration of loving as we are made to love … Honesty and repentance are pre-conditions for life,

but love sets the soul free to soar through the damage of the past and the unrequited passion of the present … forgiveness is the energy that propels the damaged man or woman toward the freedom to love.[3]

Before a sufferer is willing to allow God to be in control of her life, she may have to change the way she sees God. Our mental picture of God is often based on significant people in our childhood. The sufferer may see God as:

- angry and ready to punish
- unable to please
- over-controlling
- distant, rigid and authoritarian
- someone who's too busy to listen
- unable to cope with her emotions
- more interested in her performance than her as a person

NEW IDENTITY

In choosing to hand over the control of the eating disorder, in addition, the sufferer is choosing to let go of the eating disorder identity. One of the biggest fears for a lot of eating disorder sufferers is that if they let go of the eating disorder identity they will become a nothing and a nobody. In order to let go and not take the eating disorder identity back again, it is vital that a clear sense of identity is found. In my mind, identity has two clear components: core identity and our individual identity. Core identity defines where you have come from (and for the Christian consists of identity in Christ) and individual identity defines uniqueness as a person.

For me, some of the outer circle (the individual identity) would consist of:

- creativity
- imagination
- wisdom
- sensitivity

My core identity is that of a child of God and is completely the same as everyone else who has given their life to Christ. My core identity cannot change although my understanding of it may grow; on the other hand, my individual identity can change as I grow and develop and define my interests.

IDENTITY IN CHRIST
We are:
- a chosen people (1 Pet. 2:9)
- precious (Isa. 43:4)
- loved (1 John 4:10)
- His sons and daughters (2 Cor. 6:18)
- called (1 Thess. 5:24)
- an heir (Gal. 4:7)
- belonging to God (1 Pet. 2:9)
- honoured (Isa. 43:4)
- accepted (Rom. 15:7)
- set free (Col. 1:14, CEV)
- forgiven (Col. 3:13)

Knowing what God is really like means knowing the character of God. Some of His traits are:
- unfailing love (Psa. 36:7)
- faithful to His promises (Isa. 30:18, TLB)

- truly good (Luke 18:19, TLB)
- has compassion (Psa. 145:9)
- slow to anger (Num. 14:18)
- full of wisdom (Psa. 36:6, TLB)
- forgiving (1 John 1:9)
- rich in mercy (Eph. 2:4)
- can do anything (Job 42:2, TLB)
- does not change (James 1:17)
- full of grace and truth (John 1:14)
- tender kindness (Psa. 89:1, TLB)
- perfect in His understanding (Job 36:5, TLB)
- just and fair (Deut. 32:4, TLB)

PURSUING LIFE

With a strong sense of identity in place, it is more possible for the eating disorder sufferer to pursue life and move towards growth and maturity.

Growth must be cultivated, and in order to experience this, the sufferer needs first to recognise what prevents growth. If she has not worked through her emotional problems and is still holding onto a distorted picture of herself and of God, the result will be stunted growth. Another stumbling block is a loss of commitment to recovery. Growth is also restricted if communication is poor or if the sufferer lacks honesty and openness. 'We were created to live in relationship with others and relationships are maintained largely through communication.'[4]

Growth is a part of the path to maturity. Selwyn Hughes[5] suggests ten marks of maturity:

1. A willingness to accept the responsibility for being what we are
2. Dependent trust
3. An obedient heart
4. A willingness to face and feel everything that goes on inside us
5. A deep personal joy
6. The ability to relate to others
7. A strong sense of morality
8. A healthy sense of self-worth
9. A continued thirsting after God
10. An overflowing love

'Maturity is not the absence of struggle, but the ability to struggle well; it is not the absence of pain, but the ability to know God in the midst of pain.'[6]

Growth and maturity are working towards Jesus' words: 'Be perfect, therefore, as your heavenly Father is perfect' (Matt. 5:48). Most sufferers will interpret this as a command to be a perfectionist, failing in nothing. But the Greek word for perfection, *teleios*, is used not just in connection with goodness but with being 'complete', 'fully grown', 'mature', which, to me, signifies being 'made whole'. To overcome an eating disorder is to be 'made whole'.

'The visible evidence of maturity is relating in love. As people learn to love, the internal structures that sustain their emotional and psychological ills are eroded.'[7]

ENDURANCE

I would urge those who are struggling with overcoming an eating disorder to keep working towards *full* recovery, fuelled by the knowledge of God's great love for them. The Bible says, 'but he who perseveres and endures to the end will be saved ...' (Matt. 10:22, Amplified).

> Endurance has two aspects: on the one side it means the commitment on our part not to give up, a determination to go all the way through; on the other side it has to do with God's enablement. What God calls us to do, He gives us the grace to accomplish ... Sometimes you might feel it's impossible to go through to the end, to endure. And that may be right! But when we come to the end of what is possible for us, then we can see God do the impossible. Faith has not begun until we believe God for the impossible.[8]

The lions may grow weak
and hungry,
but those who seek the
LORD lack
no good thing ...

The *righteous* cry out, and the
LORD hears them;
he delivers them from all
their troubles.
The LORD is close to the
broken-hearted
and saves those who are crushed
in spirit.
(Psa. 34:10; 17–18, my italics)

NOTES

CHAPTER 1

1. www.wordplay.com/tourism/icebergs. Dr Stephen E. Bruneau, *Icebergs of Newfoundland and Labrador* (St John's, NL, Canada: Flanker Press Ltd, 2004).
2. *Diagnostic and Statistic Manual of Mental Disorders*, Fourth Edition Text Revision, DSM-IV-TR (American Psychiatric Association, 2000), pp.589, 594–595. Used by permission.
3. Ibid., p.787.
4. J. Yager, H.E. Gwirtsman and C.K. Edelstein (eds), *Special Problems in Managing Eating Disorders* (Washington DC: American Psychiatric Press, 1992).

CHAPTER 2

1. M. Lawrence and M. Dana, *Fighting Food* (London: Penguin, 1990).
2. Ibid., p.14.
3. Ibid., p.14.
4. C. Wills-Brandon, *Learning to Say No* (Deerfield Beach, Florida: Health Communications, 1990) p.73.
5. G. Roth, *Feeding the Hungry Heart* (London: Grafton Books, 1986).
6. Dr J. Sturt, 'Low Self-Esteem – Untangling the Roots', *Carer and Counsellor*, Vol 3, No. 2, spring 1993, p.39.
7. Ibid., p.37.
8. A.T. Beck, et al, *Cognitive Therapy of Depression* (New York: Guildford Press, 1979).
9. Dr J. Sturt, 'Low Self-Esteem – Untangling the Roots', *Carer and Counsellor*, Vol 3, No. 2, spring 1993, p.39.
10. M. Lawrence and M. Dana, *Fighting Food* (London: Penguin, 1990).
11. Dr J.H. Lacey, *A Bulimic Syndrome*, at the Sixth World Congress of the International College of Psychosomatic Medicine (Montreal, October 1981).
12. S. Orbach, *Fat is a Feminist Issue* (London: Arrow, 1986).
13. Ibid., p.94.
14. M. Woodman, *The Owl was a Baker's Daughter* (Toronto: Inner City Books, 1980).
15. A.G. Cole, 'Body and Soul: Eating Disorders as a Re-enactment

of Sexual Abuse', paper delivered at the Sexual Abuse Lecture and Workshop Series (Amber, Pennsylvania: The Horsham Clinic, November 1992) p.12.

16. The Colin A. Ross Institute For Psychological Trauma, 1701 Gateway, Suite 349, Richardson, TX 75080, USA. Used by permission. Email: rossinst@rossinst.com Web: www.rossinst.com

17. P. Lambley, *How to Survive Anorexia* ((London: Frederick Muller, 1983).

18. Ibid.

19. Ibid.

20. B.M. Dolan, et al, 'Family Features Associated with Normal Body Weight Bulimia', *International Journal of Eating Disorders*, Vol 9, No. 6, 1990.

21. M. West, *Shame-Based Family Systems* (Minneapolis, Minnesota: CompCare Publishers, 1982).

22. J. VanVonderen, *Tired of Trying to Measure Up* (Minneapolis, Minnesota: Bethany House, 1989).

23. M. Lawrence and M. Dana, *Fighting Food* (London: Penguin, 1990).

24. S. Minuchin, B.L. Rosman and L. Baker, *Psychosomatic Families: Anorexia Nervosa in Context* (Cambridge, Mass.: Harvard University Press, 1978). [Own simplified words.]

25. J. Moorey, *Living with Anorexia and Bulimia* (Manchester University Press, 1991).

26. M. Lawrence (ed), *Fed Up and Hungry* (London: The Women's Press, 1987).

27. H. Bruch, *Eating Disorders: Obesity, Anorexia Nervosa and the Person Within* (London: Routledge and Kegan Paul, 1974).

28. P.M. Smith, *The Food Trap* (Lake Mary, Florida: Creation House, 1990) pp.126, 128.

29. J. VanVonderen, *Tired of Trying to Measure Up* (Minneapolis, Minnesota: Bethany House, 1989).

CHAPTER 3

1. J. Bradshaw, *Healing the Shame that Binds You* (Deerfield Beach, Florida: Health Communications, 1988).

2. Ibid.

3. Ibid., pp.11-12.

4. P. Lambley, *How to Survive Anorexia* (London: Frederick Muller, 1983) p.188.
5. J. Welbourne and J. Purgold, *The Eating Sickness, Anorexia, Bulimia and the Myth of Suicide by Slimming* (Brighton, Sussex: Harvester Press, 1984), p.120.
6. M. Lawrence and M. Dana, *Fighting Food* (London: Penguin, 1990).
7. M. Duker and R. Slade, *Anorexia Nervosa and Bulimia: How to Help* (Milton Keynes: Open University Press, 1988).

CHAPTER 4
1. M. Dana and M. Lawrence, *Women's Secret Disorder* (London: Grafton Books, 1988), p.42.
2. Ibid.
3. Ibid., p.54.
4. Ibid., pp.59–60.
5. Ibid.
6. M. Lawrence and M. Dana, *Fighting Food* (London: Penguin, 1990), p.48.

CHAPTER 5
1. S. Billigmeier, *Inner Eating* (Nashville, Tennessee: Oliver Nelson, 1991), p. XVIII.
2. Ibid.
3. Dr J. Hollis, *Fat is a Family Affair* (Center City, Minnesota: Hazelden Educational Materials, 1985), p.33.
4. H. Bruch in P. Maisner and J. Pulling, *Feasting and Fasting* (London: Fontana, 1985).
5. Dr F. Minirth, Dr P. Meier, Dr R. Hemfelt and Dr S. Sneed, *Love Hunger* (Guildford: Highland Books, 1991) p.24.
6. P.M. Smith, *The Food Trap* (Lake Mary, Florida: Creation House, 1990) p.27.
7. S. Orbach, *Fat is a Feminist Issue* (London: Arrow, 1986) p.68.
8. Dr F. Minirth, Dr P. Meier, Dr R. Hemfelt and Dr S. Sneed, *Love Hunger* (Guildford: Highland Books, 1991).
9. M. Lawrence and M. Dana, *Fighting Food* (London: Penguin, 1990) p.62.
10. S. Orbach, *Fat is a Feminist Issue* (London: Arrow, 1986) p.85.

CHAPTER 6

1. www.wordplay.com/tourism/icebergs. Dr. Stephen E. Bruneau, *Icebergs of Newfoundland and Labrador* (St John's, NL, Canada: Flanker Press Ltd, 2004).
2. G. Roth, *Breaking Free from Compulsive Eating* (London: Grafton Books, 1986) p.176.
3. J. Welbourne and J. Purgold, *The Eating Sickness, Anorexia, Bulimia and the Myth of Suicide by Slimming* (Brighton, Sussex: Harvester Press, 1984) p.55.
4. M. Duker and R. Slade, *Anorexia Nervosa and Bulimia: How to Help* (Milton Keynes: Open University Press, 1988) p.208.
5. Dr J. Hollis, *Fat is a Family Affair* (Center City, Minnesota: Hazelden Educational Materials, 1985) p.9.
6. www.wordplay.com/tourism/icebergs. Dr Stephen E. Bruneau, *Icebergs of Newfoundland and Labrador* (St John's, NL, Canada: Flanker Press, 2004).
7. J. Yager, H.E. Gwirtsman and C.K. Edelstein (eds), *Special Problems in Managing Eating Disorders* (Washington DC: American Psychiatric Press, 1992).
8. Ibid.
9. 'New ID', a course for people struggling with eating disorders, written by Kim Hemsley. Contact Karla Brooks, St Mary's, 020 7258 5040, email: newid@stmaryslondon.com

CHAPTER 7

1. F. Heckel, *Les Grandes et Petits Obesites* (Paris: Maison et Cie, 1911).
2. G. Roth, *Breaking Free from Compulsive Eating* (London: Grafton Books, 1986) p.30.
3. S. Billigmeier, *Inner Eating* (Nashville, Tennessee: Oliver Nelson, 1991).
4. The diagrams are based on images from www.high-fiber-health.com
5. The diagrams are based on images from www.high-fiber-health.com
6. Information received from www.high-fiber-health.com

CHAPTER 8

1. E. Bass and L. Davis, *The Courage to Heal* (London: Cedar Books,

1990), p.193.

2. A. Dickson, *A Woman in Your Own Right* (London: Quartet Books, 1982).

3. Colin A. Ross, *The Trauma Model: A Solution to the Problem of Comorbidity in Psychiatry* (Richardson, Texas: Manitou Communications Paperback) December 2001. The Colin A. Ross Institute For Psychological Trauma, www.rossinst.com

4. M. Lawrence (ed), *Fed Up and Hungry* (London: The Women's Press, 1987) p.101.

5. W. Backus and M. Chapian, *Telling Yourself the Truth* (Minneapolis, Minnesota: Bethany House, 1980) p.35.

6. V. Frankl, in *Every Day with Jesus* (Farnham, Surrey: CWR, January/February 1993).

CHAPTER 9

1. Dr A. Ellis, *Reason and Emotion in Psychotherapy* (Secaucus, New Jersey: Citadel Press, 1964).

2. Don Dulaney, a social scientist from the USA.

3. Trevor Powell, *The Mental Health Handbook; Revised Edition* (Oxon: Speechmark Publishing, 2001) p.83. Adapted from Ellis and Harper, 1975.

4. Trevor Powell, *The Mental Health Handbook; Revised Edition* (Oxon: Speechmark Publishing, 2001) p.76.

5. A.T. Beck and G. Emery in J. Moorey, *Living with Anorexia and Bulimia* (Manchester University Press) p.112.

CHAPTER 10

1. Dr Neil T. Anderson, *The Bondage Breaker* (London: Monarch Books, 2000) pp.61-62.

2. L. Ogilvie, *12 Steps to Living Without Fear* (Waco, Texas: Word Books, 1987) p.133.

3. Dr D.B. Allender, *The Wounded Heart* (Farnham, Surrey: CWR, 1991) pp.181, 219.

4. M. Pytches, 'A Journey to Maturity', *The Christian Counsellor*, Vol 2, No. 3, summer 1992, p.9.

5. S. Hughes, *Every Day with Jesus* (Farnham, Surrey: CWR, January/

February 1993).

6. Helena Wilkinson interviewing Tom Varney in *The Christian Counsellor*, Vol 2, No. 3, summer 1992, p.13.

7. L. Crabb, *Understanding People* (London: Marshall Pickering, 1988) p.199.

8. F. McClung, *The Father Heart of God* (Eastbourne: Kingsway, 1985) pp.98–99.

Other books by Helena Wilkinson

Puppet on a String (Horsham, UK: RoperPenberthy Publishing, 2004)
Snakes and Ladders (RoperPenberthy Publishing – to be republished 2006)
Beyond Chaotic Eating (RoperPenberthy Publishing, 2001)
Beyond Singleness (RoperPenberthy Publishing – to be republished 2006)
Breaking Free from Loneliness (RoperPenberthy Publishing, 2004)
A Way Out of Despair (Farnham, Surrey: CWR, 1995)
Website: www.helenawilkinson.co.uk

National Distributors

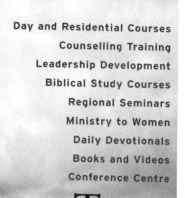

Waverley Abbey Insight Series: Insight into Self-esteem

An honest and personal approach to the problems of low self-esteem. Cultivating healthy self-esteem grows from a deepening relationship with God. The insights shared here incorporate a foundation of established research and a wealth of practical experience.

ISBN-13: 978-1-85345-409-7
ISBN-10: 1-85345-409-5
£7.50 (plus p&p)

Price correct at time of printing